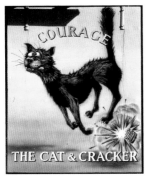

All
About
Pub Signs

Dorothy Nicolle

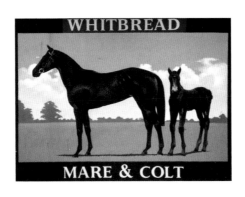

I could never have written this book without the help
and encouragement of my friends.
I particularly want to mention those who are fellow
members of the Inn Sign Society, with whom I have
been swapping pub sign pictures for many years.
There are so many of you that I couldn't possibly
list you all but I do particularly want to say a special
thank you to Alan and Carol.
Thank you, all of you.

ISBN 978-0-9560293-3-1

Published by:
Blue Hills Press, 32 Chapel Street, Wem, Shropshire SY4 5ER
www.bluehillspress.co.uk

Printed by:
Cambrian Printers, Llanbadarn Road, Aberystwyth SY23 3TN

Contents

If all be true that I do think,
There are five reasons we should drink:
Good wine – a friend – or being dry –
Or lest we should be by and by –
Or any other reason why.
Henry Aldrich (1647 - 1710),
Dean of Christ Church College, Oxford in *Reasons for Drinking*

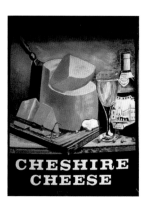

CHESHIRE CHEESE

WHITBREAD DOUBLE GLOUCESTER

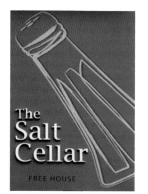

The Salt Cellar

FREE HOUSE

STAFF OF LIFE

THE BREAD & CHEESE

THE GREENGAGE

YOUNG'S

BUNCH OF GRAPES

THE PEAR & PARTRIDGE

Food, and particularly cheese, features often on pub signs.

Mousetrap

THE DEVONSHIRE DUMPLING

FREE HOUSE

REA ALES

FOOD SE ED ALL DAY

The LEG 'O' MUTTON INN

Introduction

There is nothing which has yet been contrived by man by which
so much happiness is produced as by a good tavern or inn.
Dr Johnson (1709 – 1784)

Not so long ago a poll was carried out to discover which icon best symbolised this country. People around the world, not just within the United Kingdom, were asked to make their choices and many obvious things were listed – there were red letterboxes, Big Ben, double-decker buses, the BBC, fish and chips. One icon that came near the top of everyone's list was the English pub with its pictorial pub sign.

The pub sign is very much an English, as opposed to a British, tradition as you will see as you read this book. Each of us has a favourite pub sign that we have delighted in, whether because of its historical appropriateness, its quirky name or unusual interpretation of a common name, or simply because of its sheer beauty.

Today, however, we are in danger of losing this wonderful art form. Pubs up and down the country are closing at an alarming rate; sometimes we lose as many as fifty in a week. This book has been written in the hope that it will raise awareness in the general public of what a treasure it is we are losing.

In writing this book I have had considerable support from my friends at the Inn Sign Society. I owe them thanks for their comments and for the use of many of their photos.

Dorothy Nicolle
2010

At the sign of The **Bush**

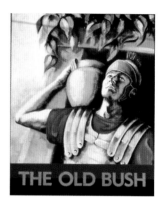

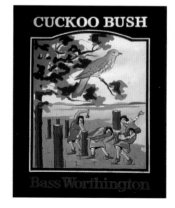

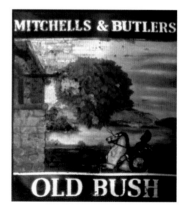

1

The earliest pub signs

He was a wise man who invented beer.
Plato (427 BC – 347 BC)

Believe it or not, our earliest pub signs date back to the time of the Roman Empire. Britain, or Britannia as it was then known, was just one province in an Empire that stretched from the British Isles to North Africa, from Spain to Syria; vastly different in terms of climate, race, you name it, this territory was ruled as one, with laws that were the same throughout the Empire. Where armies controlled and laws were foisted on subject peoples, customs soon followed. And one custom was the pub sign or, rather, the tavern sign.

It was the custom throughout the Roman Empire to have signs over different types of shops, and tavern keepers would advertise the fact that they had a new wine available for their customers by hanging some branches of a vine plant over their door. This idea was adopted by tavern keepers throughout the Empire. In Britannia, however, it wasn't generally wine that was being sold to the local people but ale and there were certainly few vine plants around for their branches to be

used. So, instead, it became the tradition to hang a branch from a bush over your door when you wanted to show that you had ale available for sale.

And so the sign of **The Bush** was born. Incidentally, this tradition has since given rise to the old saying that "a good wine (or beer) needs no bush" – in other words, it doesn't need advertising, word of mouth will be sufficient.

The Roman Empire came and went but it would appear that this tradition of hanging the branch of a bush over an alehouse in this country survived. Depicted on the *Bayeux Tapestry* there is one building that appears to have a brown pole sticking out from one corner, with a lump of green at the end of it. It's thought by many experts that this is therefore an early depiction of a Saxon alehouse with its bush sign sticking out from the building – it must be remembered that although we see the *Bayeux Tapestry* as being Norman, it was actually worked by Saxon needlewomen.

DUKE of LANCASTER

*Whosoever shall brew ale in the town with the
intention of selling it must hang out a sign,
otherwise he shall forfeit his ale.*
1393 legislation

Alehouses are places where people drink, sometimes to excess. This, inevitably, causes riotousness and bad behaviour, so it's not surprising that the authorities should want to control them. In medieval England not all houses had a branch from a bush hanging over their doors; some had signs; many had no indication at all that they were alehouses. In order to control such places you first of all need to know where they are and so, in the 1390s, a law was passed stipulating that all places selling alcohol had to have a standardised sign hanging near the door.

Imagine you are the landlord of a small alehouse – you've been told that you must put up a sign; not only are you illiterate but most of your customers are, too. So the sign you put up will be pictorial in design. But what do you put on that sign? Wanting to keep on the right side of the law you inevitably decide to use the badge of the most powerful man in the country.

This was the 1390s and, contrary to expectations, the most powerful man in the country was not the king, Richard II, but his uncle, John of Gaunt, Duke of Lancaster. Many innkeepers, alehouse landlords and the like decided to use on their sign a symbol representing John of Gaunt. Incorporated in his coat of arms was something that was instantly recognisable and relatively easy to depict and this was a red lion. Thus, the **Red Lion** became such a popular sign.

It was because this law was passed in England (and England was then an entirely separate country from Scotland, Wales or Ireland) that the pictorial pub sign became so closely associated with England and not with the rest of the nations of the British Isles. It's really only in the last fifty years or so that pictorial signs have become at all common outside of England. Hence this is definitely an English, rather than a British, tradition.

It wasn't just John of Gaunt's association with the sign of the red lion that made it so popular. Just over 200 years later the Queen of England, Elizabeth I, died and was succeeded by James VI of Scotland. Once again, landlords up and down the country wanted to be seen to be supporting the new regime, so that many of them adopted an easily recognisable Scottish symbol for their pub signs – and there was once again a surge in popularity for naming pubs the Red Lion. Thus, today, this is one of the most common signs wherever you go; there's hardly a town in the country without a Red Lion pub somewhere.

THE RED LION

Mitchells & Butlers

Red Lion

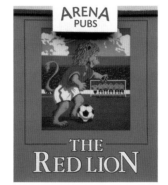

ARENA PUBS

THE RED LION

THE RED LION

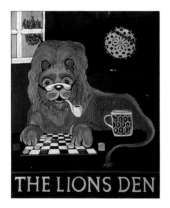

THE LIONS DEN

BLACK LION

CHARRINGTON

BRITISH LION

The **Lettered Board**
All ye who thirst, come enter here
And tarry while ye will
For we have cheer and good strong ale
So come and drink your fill.

Once the signs had been erected it was easy for the authorities in each town and village to see where the alehouses were, so that they could control the drunks who issued from them. It meant, also, that they were now able to check the quality of the ale that was being produced and it's from this period that we see the emergence of the "ale taster" going from alehouse to alehouse to check the quality of the brews. Perhaps the best known of them was William Shakespeare's father, John Shakespeare, who was an ale-taster or "conner" in Stratford-upon-Avon in the 1500s.

In an age without scientific instruments accurate measurements of strength were not possible, so that one method was to test for the amount of sugar in the wort before fermentation. Wort is liquid extracted during the brewing process and contains the sugars which, when the brew is fermented, will produce the alcohol. The greater the sugar content, the greater the alcohol content (and the more duty that can subsequently be imposed on the brewer!).

It's these sugars that subsequently produce the alcohol in the brew. Therefore testing the amount of sugar at this point gives a fair indication of its final strength. The higher the sugar content the stickier it was and so an unusual method of testing developed – wort would be poured over a stool which the ale tester would sit on for a time. The strength of the wort was then determined according to how much it stuck to the taster's breeches once he got up.

Adam's ale is the best brew.
Proverb
– mind you, this refers to water, not ale!

Pub names are often being changed as new landlords take over. Occasionally, however, a pub name will change as a result of local usage as, for example, when a nickname takes over as an official name. The heraldic term for a red lion standing on its hind legs, head in profile, is that it is "rampant" and this is probably the origin of the sign The **Romping Cat**.

In AD 975 King Edgar tried to curb ale consumption throughout the country. Ale at this time was often drunk from large tankards which would be passed from one person to the next, each man taking his fair share. A system was introduced whereby wooden pegs were stuck onto the tankards to mark one pint measures and no man was therefore allowed to drink more than one measure. Of course the system never worked as people inevitably drank beyond the measure. This is thought to be where we get the saying "to take a person down a peg or two".

2

The earliest pubs and breweries

The innkeeper loves the drunkard, but not as a son-in-law.
Jewish proverb

Beers have been drunk for millennia in one form or another. The ancient Egyptians refer to the drink in medical prescriptions for their god, Osiris. There's what appears to be an old malt kiln on the Neolithic site of Skara Brae on Orkney, indicating that brewing was taking place there some 5,000 years ago. Then there's evidence, too, of a brewery producing ale for the Roman soldiers living along Hadrian's Wall from around 120 AD.

In medieval times brewing ale was predominantly women's work. Ale was an essential part of the daily diet of everyone at the time and the housewives would produce it along with any food to be consumed within their households. Inevitably, some housewives brewed a better ale than others and they would then often make it in greater quantities in order to sell the surplus and increase their income. And so the first alehouses developed and, at this time in history, it was invariably women who ran them.

People drank ale in vast quantities – it's said that the average man probably drank at least a gallon each day. There's one reference to the ladies-in-waiting at the court of King Henry VIII being allowed a gallon of beer for breakfast alone. But when the purity of the water could never be guaranteed, it was the one drink that was safe. And it was nutritious, too, providing many people with much of their required B-vitamins, protein and carbohydrate.

Queen Elizabeth I used to take ale with her breakfast – she preferred an ale that wasn't too strong known as "single" ale or "small beer". Apparently, before setting off on one of her travels around the country, she would always send people ahead to check the quality of the ales. If they weren't good enough she would then ensure that a supply from London was sent ahead for her.

Kings Head

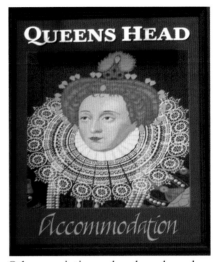

There are so many different terms for ales and beers that it can become most confusing, particularly when they are used interchangeably. The Old English word "ale" was the name given by the Anglo-Saxons to any fermented drink that was brewed from malted grain and water. The grain used most often was barley although, in the north of Britain oats were used and, in some localised areas, wheat or even beans.

"Beer" (from the Latin *biber*, to drink) was also occasionally used to refer to the same drink. This changed, however, in the 1500s when beer came to refer to a different drink altogether. By then hops were being added to the brew and it was this drink, with hops used as flavouring, that came to be called "beer" as opposed to "ale".

Traditionally ales had been brewed in different strengths so that there are references in medieval times to "small beer" (a single strength beer), "double beer" (a strong beer) and "double-double" (the strongest). Queen Elizabeth I tried to stop production of "double-double" in 1560, not that she was successful.

Hopped beer, when it was introduced, was an acquired taste, being rather bitter by comparison with the old ales – hence it also came to be known as "bitter". Other variations developed such as "porter" (a mixture of three beers, apparently so-called because it was a favourite of London porters), and "stout" (a stronger blend). "Lager" is beer that can be stored for a time before consumption – the word comes from the German meaning "to store", "lagerbier" being beer that matured in the barrel before being drunk. Today "beer" is often used as a generic term for all of the above.

Alewives had been playing with their recipes for years, introducing herbs, spices and fruits so that, alongside the development of the new breweries, many of these cottage industries continued to thrive. Some of the names for these old drinks are wonderful – Lamb's Wool (with soft baked apples in it), Cock Ale (chicken and raisins) and buttered ales with butter, sugar and cinnamon in the recipe. It's a tradition that continues to this day with home-brewers making their own beers and branching out into drinks like elderberry wines. Mind you, many alewives also adulterated

Hole in the Wall
- pubs with this name often started life as small cottage breweries which served their drink through an open window.

their drinks with resin or salt or even chicken droppings – this last apparently thickened the brew nicely.

While on the subject of names for different drinks, the term "booze", a general term for all drinks, comes from the Dutch *buizen* meaning "to drink to excess" and goes back probably to the 1600s. "Plonk" dates only to the time of the First World War. Soldiers serving in the trenches would get local leave and, wanting to order the cheapest drinks in the French bars, would try to say *vin blanc*. "Punch" is thought to date back to the 1700s and employees serving in India with the East India Company – it was a mixed drink, traditionally using five ingredients (spirit, water, spices, sugar and fruit juice) and comes from an Indian word meaning "five".

The confusion over words such as ale, beer, lager and so on also applies to the use of terms such as alehouse, pub, tavern, inn… Many of the terms are obvious – an alehouse or a beerhouse sold ale or beer, just as a tea shop or wine bar today sell tea or wine. A "tavern", from the Latin *taberna*, was originally a place that sold wine in the time of the Roman Empire. It developed into a place that sold a selection of drinks including wine and ales or beers. A "bar" is a barrier, in other words it just refers to the table between the landlord and his customer over which the drinks are sold. Your "local" is, of course, the drinking house in your local area, the one that you frequent.

The term "pub" or "public house" developed in Tudor times. As always, the authorities wanted control over such places and the drunken and rowdy people who used them. Consequently, in 1495 during the reign of Henry VII, a law was passed stipulating that all people selling alcohol had to be prepared to have government officials check their premises on a regular basis. Hence such buildings came under public control, hence public houses. Subsequently, in 1552 a further law was passed making it necessary for all alehouse keepers to obtain a licence. Although there are numerous pubs around the country that can genuinely claim to be much older, it's from around this time that we really start to get official records of such places being run as pubs.

All the above places sold drink; many of them also sold food. An "inn", however, was an establishment that sold not only food and drink but also provided accommodation, often not only for human customers but for their horses, too.

Incidentally, many visitors to our shores are delighted at the prospect of a free drink when they see the word "Freehouse" over a pub's entrance. Sadly for them, this simply indicates that the landlord is independent, that is "free" from the outside control of a brewery.

The **Vintage**

The **Sun Inn** at Leintwardine. This is a "parlour inn" and hearkens back to early days when an alewife would invite people into her home to consume the ale she had brewed. Very few survive today.

The **Cider Press** – in some areas it was cider, rather than ale, that was the dominant drink. Laws governing one also applied to the other and many pub signs remind us of the importance of this local drink.

Battle Cruiser – Cockney rhyming slang has also played its part in giving nicknames for pubs. Here "cruiser" obviously rhymes with boozer. Others include "Rub-a-dub-dub" and "Nuclear Sub" both of which rhyme with pub.

I feel no pain, dear mother, now
But oh, I am so dry!
O take me to a brewery
And leave me there to die.
Shanty

For centuries ale was brewed on a small scale. The drink had a short shelf-life so that it was never commercially viable to produce it in large

The **Brewer's Delight**

The oldest established brewery in the country is Shepherd Neame's in Kent. It's perhaps no surprise, therefore, that it was also in Kent that hops were first grown, being introduced in the early 1500s by Flemish immigrants. Mind you, the Brewer's Company at the time deplored this new custom of adding hops to ale, saying that anyone who added "any hoppes, herbs or other like thing but only licquor, malt and yeste" should be outlawed.

quantities. The introduction of hops, however, changed all this. Hops had preservative qualities enabling the brewer to produce much more beer at any one time, knowing that it would keep for longer. Thus, it was in the 16th century that we get the beginnings of breweries in the modern sense – producers of large quantities of beer for consumption not only on the premises but being sold on to inns and pubs for consumption elsewhere.

To produce ale or beer the barley first needs to be soaked for several days to encourage it to germinate. It is then dried to prevent further germination – this is the malting process. Once dried, the barley is milled down and mixed with hot water. The mixture is left to stand for up to two hours, which is when the sugars in the barley are released. The liquid sugar (or "wort") is then separated from the spent grains and this was generally used for animal feed. (It was at this point, in the past, that the wort would be tested by the ale-conner or aletaster.) Once the wort has cooled, yeast is added and it's all left to ferment before hops or other flavourings are added and the mixture is finally ready for drinking. (These days the beers are also usually pasteurised, which adds to their shelf-life too.)

It's a tedious process so that perhaps it's little wonder that once the breweries began to be established they quickly took trade from the individual alewife.

Beer brewers shall sell no beer to the citizens
unless it be three weeks old; to the foreigner they
may knowingly sell younger beer.
German beer law, 1466

JOLLY BREWER

THE TWO BREWERS

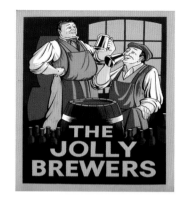

THE JOLLY BREWERS

THE MALTSTERS

Remember: "I" before "E", except in Budweiser.
Anon

Pub signs linked to the brewing industry.

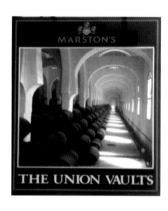

THE UNION VAULTS

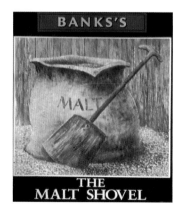

THE MALT SHOVEL

MALT SHOVEL

MALT SHOVEL

3
Pubs and the church

A cask of wine works more miracles than a church full of saints.
Proverb

Throughout medieval England there were numerous small pubs, inns and alehouses. Housewives usually brewed ale for all the members of their household and in large establishments there would have been brewhouses used solely for this purpose.

It seems strange to us today but, over and above all these ale producers, the one group in the country that easily produced the most ale was the church. I'm speaking here not of individual churches but of all the monastic establishments up and down the country with their numerous monks and laybrothers (not to mention, all the convents with their nuns, too). But they weren't the only people living in such places – abbeys were also places where the sick were tended, where the sons of nobles and merchants went to be educated, where orphaned children were raised and where the elderly saw out their last days. Travellers moving around the country would invariably look for accommodation in abbeys. All these people had to be catered for and doing this required vast quantities of food and drink. Ale was produced in almost industrial quantities and, to this day, you will find inns with names that reflect this link to a local abbey or priory.

GOOD MIXER

THE FRIARS' TAVERN

THE PARSONS' NOSE

AN ENTERPRISE INNS FREE HOUSE

MERRIE MONK

GREENE KING

WHO'D A THOUGHT IT

WADWORTH

The best beer is where priests go to drink.
William Shakespeare (1564 – 1616)
A Winter's Tale

Producing ale in such quantities also required a degree of quality-control. It was therefore in monastic brewhouses and cellars that a system of defining the strength of ale was developed. Casked ale would be tasted and the casks then marked with one, two or three crosses according to their strength. Hence a weak brew or "small beer" came to be known as "single" ale. Casks holding an average strength beer were marked with two crosses and a really strong beer would have three crosses marked on the cask. Anything stronger came to be known as "double-double" and it was the production of this that was banned in 1560. (Incidentally, it's from this

Who'd a Thought It – notice the man's T-shirt reads "6X" – Wadworths Brewery in Wiltshire is famous for its 6X beer, the implication being that it's so strong that "who'd a thought it" possible.

system that the Australian trade name for XXXX beer derived but I would very much doubt whether it compares in strength with the original medieval version.)

While on the subject of casks – these came in various sizes, according to the quantities they held and, like large wine bottles, different names were given to the different size barrels. The word "cask" means a container; it comes from a Spanish word *cascara* meaning "tree bark", in the sense that the bark surrounds and holds the tree in the way that a cask surrounds and holds the beer. Just to confuse you – when empty a cask traditionally was called a "keg". A cask could be any size, while a "barrel" contained a set amount, traditionally around 36 gallons (163 litres).

Barrels are large items to carry around so that ale was often transported in "firkins". This derives from a Dutch word that meant "fourth" – so a firkin held a fourth of a full-size barrel, (nine gallons). A "tun", meantime, held around 216 gallons but this term was more often used for a barrel of wine rather than ale or beer. Just to confuse you further, when used to hold wine rather than beer a firkin then was a third of a tun.

Ale would often be brewed for consumption on special occasions or on holy days (from where we get the term "holiday"). Because so many such occasions were connected with events in the church, these often came to be known as "church ales" and they included Easter-ales, Whitsun-ales, wedding-ales and even christening-ales. Producing special ales for special occasions is a tradition continued by many breweries to this day.

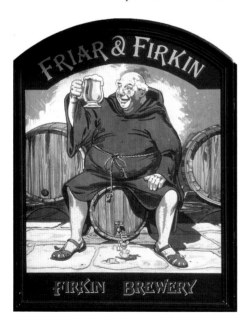

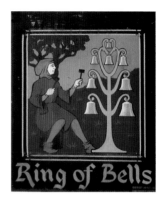

Bells come in all shapes and sizes as you can see from the examples here. Incidentally, pubs with signs denoting several bells can occasionally have a nautical association. For example a pub called the **Five Bells** in a coastal town could be reminding customers that the pub will open at 2.30 in the afternoon.

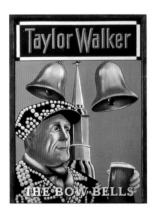

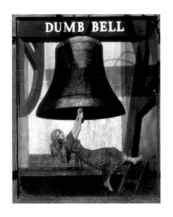

The association of the church with ale survives in numerous pub signs. Such signs include angels, mitres, abbeys, churches and so on. Pubs called the **Bell** have an obvious church link. Church bells are large, heavy and easily damaged when being transported along the poor quality roads that existed at the time. What often happened, therefore, was that the bell founders would make the bell on site, staying at the local inn while they did so and the inn would adopt the new name to commemorate the erection of the new bell or bells.

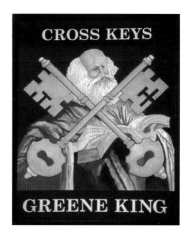

Don't automatically assume that a pub called the **Bull** has something to do with cattle. Obviously if it sits beside a former cattle market or is in cattle-rearing country this is the most likely explanation. However, you will sometimes find a Bull Inn that seems to have no such link and, instead, sits beside the entrance of a former abbey. In such cases the name may derive from a "Papal Bull" given by the Pope to an early abbot allowing the abbot to run an inn for visitors.

Original Keys

Saints feature regularly on pub signs, but not always by name. St Peter, for example, held the keys to the gates of Heaven so that any pub called the **Keys** or the **Cross Keys** is showing a direct reference to him. This association with saints and their symbols is everywhere. It's something that our ancestors would have automatically understood but, today, most of these symbolic references go completely over our heads. Others include pubs called the **Eagle** – often a direct reference to St John (the Evangelist) rather than to any bird of prey. St John's Gospel in *The Bible* begins with the words "In the beginning was the word, and the word was God …"; and, of course,

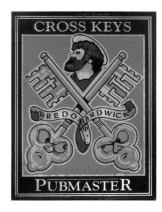

Catherine
Wheel

Lamb

readings from *The Bible* were made in churches by someone standing at a lectern frequently carved in the shape of an eagle, a reference to this gospel. Then a pub called the **Lamb** may well be referring to St John the Baptist; a **Wheel** could refer to St Catherine and there are many others.

Some saints are depicted on signs to represent local trades. **Bishop Blaize**, for example, is the patron saint of wool-combers and **Crispin**, the saint for cobblers. Other saints include **St Helena** who was the mother of the Emperor Constantine; she converted to Christianity and went travelling to the Bible Lands seeking out mementos of Jesus Christ. It's on her that we can probably put much of the blame for the enormous quantity of bits of the true cross (enough to build a medieval battleship) to be found in churches all around the world. Perhaps because of her keenness in collecting old artefacts, she became the patron saint of archaeologists. **St Nicholas**, the patron saint of children, needs no introduction. But the saint who is found most often is, not surprisingly, St George, with or without his dragon. And, finally, there are the stories from *The Bible* that survive in pub signs, even in this atheistic age, my favourite of which has to be the **Adam and Eve**, pictured here.

Give strong drink to the desperate
and wine to the embittered;
such men will drink and forget their poverty
and remember their trouble no longer.
Proverbs 31: 6-7

BISHOP BLAIZE

The ST. HELENS

THE MANSFIELD BREWERY COMPANY

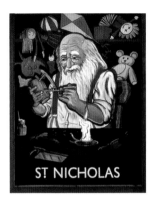

ST NICHOLAS

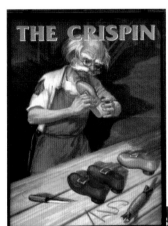

THE CRISPIN

s Charrington

Lamb & Lion

THE NOAH'S ARK

The **Noah's Ark**

*The wine had such ill effects on
Noah's health that it was all he
could do to live 950 years. Just
nineteen years short of Methuselah.
Show me a total abstainer that ever
lived that long.*
Will Rogers (1879 - 1935)

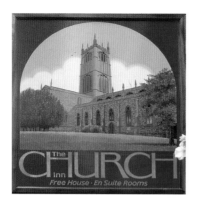

The variety of signs showing links with the church is endless. Even the Devil gets a mention - there are numerous explanations for the name **Mardol**, below. It's the name of a street in Shrewsbury and is thought to derive from the Devil in some way but no-one seems to be able to agree just how - on the pub sign it is translated as the "Devil's Limit".

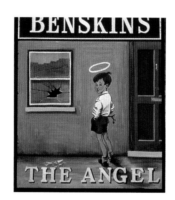

THE STONE CROSS

The Golden Cross Hotel

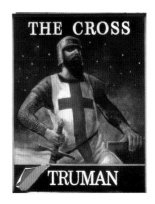

THE CROSS

TRUMAN

Ye Olde Six Bells

The Ring o'Bells

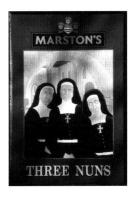

MARSTON'S

THREE NUNS

The **Sun**

*There is nothing better under the sun for man than
to eat, drink, and be merry. Go, therefore, eat your
bread with joy and drink your wine with cheer.*
Ecclesiastes 8:15
Presumably this is the origin of the saying
regarding "the best beer under the sun".

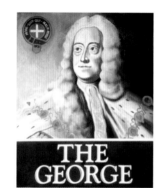

St George, he was for England
And before he killed that dragon
He drank a pint of English ale
Out of an English flagon.

When added together all the **St George**, **George and Dragon**, **King George** and **Royal George** pubs are easily the most popular name group in the country.

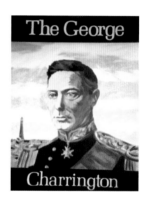

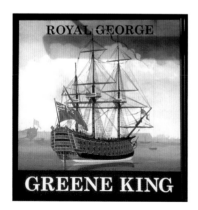

4
Royal pub signs

For a quart of Ale is a dish for a King.
William Shakespeare (1564 – 1616) *A Winter's Tale*

From the time that it first became law to hang a sign indicating the presence of an alehouse, many of the symbols on them showed references to monarchs. This was an obvious step, as showing loyalty to one's rulers was a way of keeping on the right side of the law. Similarly, many alehouses would have shown symbols associated with the local land owners and, to begin with, this included many religious symbols – the church owned something in the region of a third of the land in the country in the period leading up to Henry VIII's dissolution of the monasteries. Following the takeover of all this land it became, for many, politically expedient to change a religious sign and, once again, many people would then have adopted royal symbols for their signs, as a safe option.

Today, some 500 years later, numerous monarchs still adorn our signs or, at the very least, symbols associated with them. Along with the **King's Head** or the **Queen's Head**, the **Crown** is one of the most common pub signs in the country.

Other symbolic royal symbols include **The Ball** and the **Royal Standard**.

King's Head signs represent kings from all periods of history although Henry VIII is undoubtedly the most common. Just about any former king has been portrayed at one time or another – from (the possibly legendary) King Arthur to any of our six King Georges; there are Kings Harold, Richard, Henry, William … Not all the signs are historically accurate, however. King

KING & QUEEN

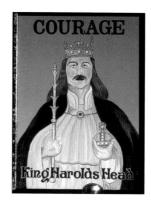

Kings and Queens
of England
through
the centuries.

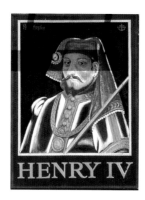

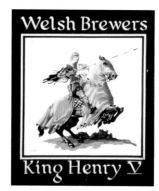

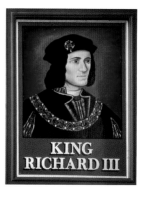

Offa is described on one sign as "King of all the English" – he wasn't.

Occasionally, there are other interpretations of the sign as with an example showing the King of Clubs from a pack of cards and I particularly like the sign below referring to the execution of King Charles I. There's a similar sign in Stratford showing a queen being executed and her head being held aloft by the executioner.

Royalist signs suffered a setback in the 1600s during the period of the Civil War and the Commonwealth that followed. Then, with the return of Charles II in 1660 they made a comeback as, yet again, it became politically expedient to show that you supported the returned, royalist regime. It so happened that Charles II arrived back in England on the 29 May, Oak Apple Day and, by this time, everyone had heard all about his exploits after the Battle of Worcester when he had hidden in an oak tree to avoid capture by the Parliamentary army. Almost overnight a new pub sign, the **Royal Oak**, appeared everywhere and this sign is another of the most popular signs today.

Incidentally, one or two signs recall that short time when this country was a republic – the **Oliver Cromwell** is an obvious example.

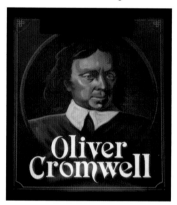

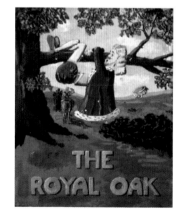

Although the royals are a popular subject for pub signs you won't see many portraits of living members of the royal family, although there are indeed one or two. This tradition dates back to the time of Queen Victoria. The story goes that she was one day visiting a town and noticed a pub sign portrait of herself that she took an instant dislike to. Returning to London she ensured that Parliament passed a law banning the portrayal of living members of the royal family. This law has never been repealed so that, technically, it is illegal to have such a sign.

In fact, no such law was ever passed so that this story is simply a myth. However, there is no doubt that Victoria, had she been displeased by a portrait of herself, would certainly have made her feelings known so that from then onwards it has been considered poor taste to show a living royal on a pub sign – not that that has stopped it entirely.

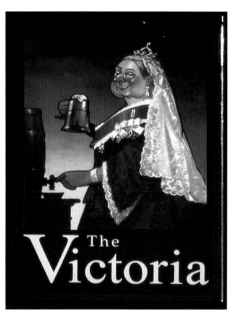

Champagne and orange juice is a great drink.
The orange improves the champagne. The
champagne definitely improves the orange.
Philip, Duke of Edinburgh

There are some wonderful royal pub signs depicting not just well-known royals but, occasionally, quite obscure members of the royal family. They include numerous almost-forgotten consorts from medieval times. Henry VIII's queens often feature. From the Hanoverian period we get **Queen Adelaide** (wife of George II), Charlotte (wife of George III) and the **Queen Dowager** (widow of William IV). But the most popular consort is male – **Prince Albert**.

The Grand Old **Duke of York** of nursery rhyme fame is there. Another obscure member of the royal family is the **Duke William** – an obvious reference to Duke William of Normandy, William the Conqueror you would think, but not necessarily although he, too, certainly has been depicted. One Duke William sign depicts William, Duke of Cumberland – or Butcher Cumberland as he came to be known in Scotland as a result of his ruthlessness is hunting down Jacobite rebels following the Battle of Culloden.

Finally, even some foreign royals have managed to find recognition on British pub signs.

*One not only drinks the wine, one smells it,
observes it, tastes it, sips it and –
one talks about it.*
King Edward VII (1901 - 1910)

QUEEN ELEANOR

THE QUEEN PHILLIPPA

YORKSHIRE ROSE

ELIZABETH OF YORK

Anne Boleyn Hotel

Queen Adelaide

YOUNG'S

QUEEN DOWAGER

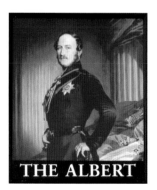

THE ALBERT

ROSE of DENMARK

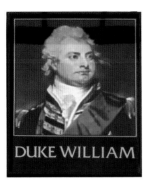

DUKE WILLIAM

SIR HARRY'S

DUCHESS OF KENT

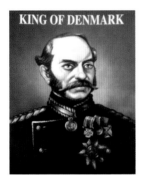

KING OF DENMARK

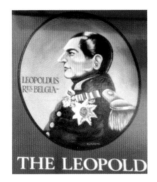

THE LEOPOLD

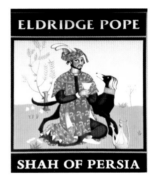

ELDRIDGE POPE

SHAH OF PERSIA

KING OF BOHEMIA

The **Cat and Fiddle** – this is an odd sign, at least so far as its derivation is concerned. It's impossible to date the earliest reference here. Although the nursery rhyme wasn't written down until sometime in the 18th century there were pubs of that name long before. Some say this is a reference to Henry VIII's first wife, Catherine of Aragon, Catherine the Faithful or *Catherine la Fidele* but the earliest reference to a pub of this name pre-dates their divorce by many years so that we just cannot explain either the rhyme or the pub name with any certainty.

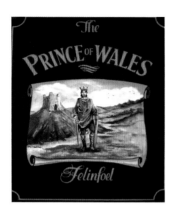

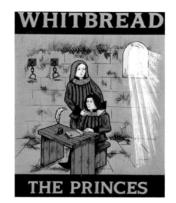

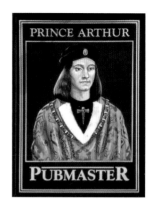

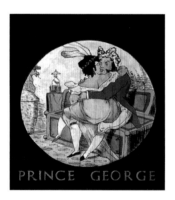

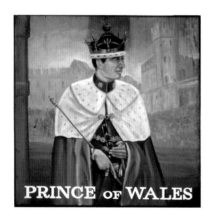

The **Prince of Wales**
The eldest of the two "**Princes** in the Tower" did become King Edward V when his father died but he had, of course, already disappeared into the Tower of London by then and history has argued ever since as to who killed him. **Prince Arthur** died before his father and so never became king; he was the first husband of Catherine of Aragon.

Symbols of State come in all forms although the **Crown** is the most obvious example and is, in fact, one of our more common names for pubs around the country.

THE BALL

GOLDEN BALL

The **King's Arms**

5
Heraldic pubs signs

Drink to nobody that you think is better than yourself.
Hannah Woolley – 17th century expert on etiquette in her
Guide to ladies, gentlewomen and maids

Although it became law in the 1390s that those people selling ale had to display a sign over their door, it was already by then common practice for many landlords. In an illiterate age a sign over the entrance to your shop indicated to the general public what goods you were selling – this survives today, for example, with the barber-surgeon's red and white pole or a pawnbroker's golden balls. So that a bush or a spray of foliage over the door had long been an indicator that ale was available on the premises.

Once it became law that a pictorial sign had to be displayed, there arose the problem of just what to depict on that sign. We have already seen how the **Red Lion** rose to prominence right from the beginning because of landlords wanting to curry favour with the power behind the throne, John of Gaunt, Duke of Lancaster. Similarly, in individual towns and villages up and down the country, it would have been a local worthy with whom it was wise to keep on good terms.

A local landowner's coat of arms, however, could show a great deal of detail and there would be no surer way of incurring his displeasure than to get a small part wrong. Consequently, many inn signs would depict a single detail from a coat of arms, something that was easily identifiable as belonging to the leading local family, and use just that. The choice of such a detail was often made very much easier because retainers working for the family would wear just such an emblem from their lord's badge prominently displayed on their coats. Hence you get signs such as the **Bear and Ragged Staff** for the Earls of Warwick (also used on the county's coat of arms) or the **Talbot** dog representing the

Earls of Shrewsbury. Incidentally, the talbot was a breed of hunting dog but the breed has now died out. This may go some way to explain why, on various signs, it can look totally different; it was the ancestor of the modern foxhound.

Taking this theme of choosing just one item from a coat of arms as the name for your pub does also mean that there can be a variety of signs of widely differing subjects that all relate to just one local family. One example is to be found in Shropshire where the Corbet family was given large estates following their arrival in England with William the Conqueror. Look at a sign for an inn called the **Corbet Arms** and you will see depicted on it a **Raven**, an **Elephant and Castle** and a **Squirrel** – all of which have been used as names for inns within the county and which indicate an allegiance in times past to this particular family. But, beware – a Raven pub in Shropshire may indicate a link to this family; in other parts of the country it was, in the 18th century, sometimes an indication that the landlord was a secret Jacobite sympathiser. Meanwhile, the Elephant and Castle was also adopted as the sign of the Cutler's Guild so that, in London at least, this may be behind the use of this sign.

Eagle and Child – this comes from the badge of the Earls of Derby, the Stanley family. Once upon a time, so the story goes, there was a Stanley whose wife was sadly unable to bear him the son and heir he so desired. However, he had a mistress who, unknown to his wife, produced a male child leaving him with the problem of how to persuade his wife to accept the child as their heir. Accordingly, Stanley got one of his retainers to take the baby into the forest and leave it on the ground beneath a tree in which there was an eagle's nest. He and his wife then went for a walk in the forest and "found" the crying baby. It was obvious to the wife what had happened – an eagle had stolen the baby and then dropped it to the ground below its nest. She turned to her husband and tearfully exclaimed that God had heard her prayers; she begged her husband to adopt the child as their own. After a great deal of persuasion Stanley finally agreed to accept the child as their son!

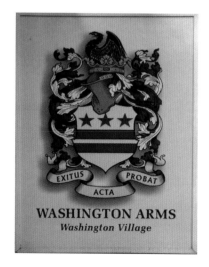

The **Washington Arms** – if this coat of arms, with its stars and stripes, reminds you of something else, then it's probably because it was the inspiration behind the flag of the USA. This is, in fact, the coat of arms of the family of George Washington.

Indeed, heraldic signs traditionally represented all scales of people from monarchs and nobility to the guilds of differing working groups and trades. A number of these inn signs survive as coats of arms; this seems to be particularly the case for some reason with pubs called the **Butchers Arms**. Today, it's just as likely that a pub named for a trade coat of arms will depict someone working at that trade rather than the coat of arms itself, as seen with some of the examples in the next chapter.

The church, too, wasn't without its heraldic signs. One name that survives is the **Lamb and Flag**, from the coat of arms of the Knights Templar, a religious order responsible for protecting pilgrims travelling to the Holy Land. The lamb refers to the Lamb of God although today the flag depicted is most likely to be the (much later) Union Flag.

The **White Horse** had been used in so many different ways on heraldic signs through the ages that today a pub with that name can represent almost anyone. In Kent it is a symbol for the county. Indeed, using that name in Kent was for a long time almost a quiet act of rebellion. Following the Battle of Hastings in 1066, William the Conqueror was in such haste to reach London and subsequently conquer the rest of England that he ignored Kent tucked away in its corner, so that the people of Kent will tell you that they were never conquered; and to call your pub the White Horse was to remind everyone of the fact.

Going further back in time, a white horse was a symbol of early Kings of Wessex; if a white horse is galloping (not very often seen on signs, I agree) it represented Hanover in Germany. But it also was used to indicate a number of different trade guilds including coachmen, farriers, saddlers, wheelwrights and, most important in this context, innkeepers.

And then, of course, there are the royal coats of arms. These can be quite detailed and vary considerably according to which monarch they represent. The supporter holding one side of the shield is usually the lion of England. On the opposite side a dragon indicates one of our Tudor monarchs; this then changed to the unicorn with the arrival of King James I in 1603. Signs with royal coats of arms have been frequently changed over the years but occasionally, as with the Tudor signs, the older versions survive. One Kings Arms sign, for example, has supporters in the form of two white boars – the white boar was the badge of the Duke of York who came to the throne as Richard III. He was defeated at the Battle of Bosworth Field in 1485 at which point it became expedient for anyone with a white boar sign to rapidly change it. It just so happened that fighting for the victor of that battle, Henry VII, was the Earl of Oxford whose badge was the blue boar so that, in the days that followed the battle, many a white boar was painted blue.

Finally, the **Plume of Feathers**, badge of the Prince of Wales, appears often. This symbol dates back to 1346 and the Battle of Crécy during which a French army was defeated by Edward, Prince of Wales, the son of King Edward III, and better known as the Black Prince. Though totally blind, King John of Bohemia insisted on fighting for the French at that battle and was, inevitably, killed. Edward, however, was so impressed by King John's courage that he adopted the old king's device of the three ostrich feathers for his own.

I am as drunk as a lord, but then, I am one,
so what does it matter.
Bertrand Russell (1872 - 1970)

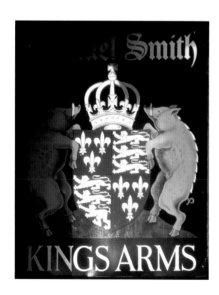

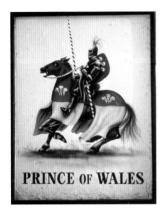

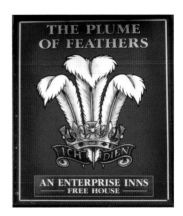

The three lions of England, the **Shrewsbury Arms** and **Loggerheads**

The three lions as a symbol of England (pictured here on a sign for the **Ashes** cricketing trophy), were adopted in the reign of Richard the Lionheart. Originally, the lion in heraldry was always shown in profile. These lions are shown in full but with their faces looking straight at you and this, in heraldic terminology, was described as "lion leopardé".

This has given rise to some confusion with Shrewsbury's coat of arms. It depicts three cat's heads which, on some signs, look like lions and on others look much more like leopards and, because the badge is very early, no-one knows just which animal it should actually be. This gave rise to a nickname for the sign of **Loggerheads**, supposedly a pun on "Leopard's heads" – perhaps the joke was more obvious when spoken in the dialect of medieval England.

To say someone is a loggerhead is to say he's a fool. The sign for **We Three Loggerheads** invariably shows only two people, the point being that anyone who asks why there are only two on the sign is showing he's a fool for not understanding the meaning, thereby becoming the third loggerhead.

THE WHITE LION

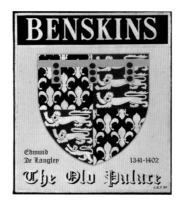

BENSKINS

Edmund De Langley 1341-1402

The Old Palace

A.R.T 89

LE·BON·TEMPS·VIENDRA

THE HARCOURT ARMS

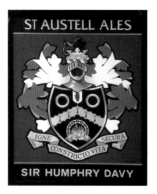

ST AUSTELL ALES

IGNE SECURA CONSTRICTO VITA

SIR HUMPHRY DAVY

Examples of Coats of Arms.

These can represent all sorts. Royal coats of arms are frequently to be found on pub signs as well as those of noble families, but there are also many coats of arms recalling individual people or trading groups.

THREE GOATS HEADS

The **EAGLES**

BUTCHERS ARMS

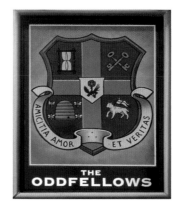

AMICITIA AMOR ET VERITAS

THE ODDFELLOWS

6
The world of work

Too much work and no vacation,
Deserves at least a small libation.
So hail! my friends, and raise your glasses;
Work's the curse of the drinking classes.
Oscar Wilde (1854 - 1900)

Trade signs on inns and alehouses were important from early medieval times. Firstly, they indicated places where people of a particular trade knew they could meet like-minded people with common interests. Also, for those people visiting an area new to them and wishing to work in a particular line of business, or else wishing to trade, it was the open door required in order to meet the right people.

Consequently, from the beginning many alehouses catered for specific trades and this is reflected in numerous signs. The wool trade, for example, brought immense wealth to the country and signs that remind us of this include the **Fleece** and the **Woolpack**, not to mention quite a few **Sheep** or **Lamb** pubs.

With so many people working in agricultural trades to provide food, agricultural signs can be found everywhere, and not just in rural areas. Signs here include the **Harrow**, the **Farmer's Boy**, even the **Farm**, the **Barley Mow** and the **Pound** (an enclosure where animals were kept). And, of course, there's the **Plough** – this sign is often depicted in the form of the

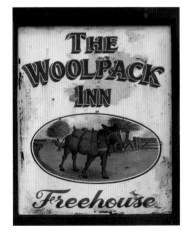

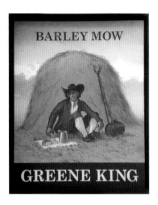

The **Farmyard** and other signs associated with agriculture.

astronomical group of stars known as the Plough and, sometimes, a pub called the **Seven Stars** would have been referring obliquely to the same thing.

Horses were used both for agricultural purposes and to support people in all walks of life, so it is not surprising that there are many references to these animals and the people who worked with them, on pub signs. Signs here include the **Farriers**, the **Anvil** and the numerous **Horseshoe** pubs.

Many dominant trades formed guilds, which in turn gave them more clout in their business dealings. Smaller trades would then find it increasingly difficult to compete on the open market and so would often band together to form their own guild of "odd" trades – hence the **Oddfellows Arms**.

Wheatsheaf – it's harvest time and the crop has been brought in, leaving sheaves of wheat in the field to be collected later. A wheatsheaf, in heraldry, symbolises plenty.

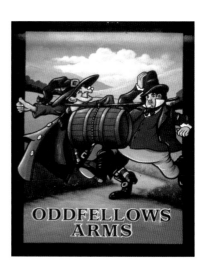

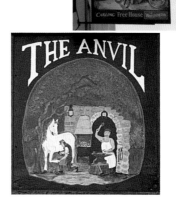

Old trades remembered on pub signs.

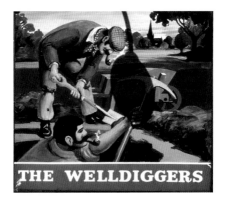

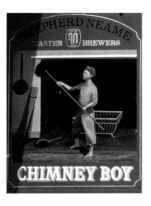

Cabbage Hall – each trade has its own language. Sometimes a tailor was given a length of cloth with which to produce six suits; with careful cutting he might be able to have enough spare cloth to produce a seventh suit – this, in the tailoring trade, was known as "cabbage". Here we see a tailor working away on his cabbage and dreaming of the castle that one day this additional income will bring him – you can see the castle through the window behind him.

Then, with the advent of the Industrial Revolution in the 18th century the variety of trades represented grew enormously. Occasionally you will come across a sign that isn't quite what it seems to represent - the **Blue Pig** is an example. Does this refer to the rearing of pigs, though why should it be blue? Or is it heraldic? In fact it is a reference to the iron industry – molten iron would be poured to form small ingots known as "pigs" that would appear to turn blue as they cooled.

THE BLUE PIG

CHARRINGTON

COOPERS APPRENTICE

The **Apprentice** – the saying "to wet your whistle" goes back a long way, being used by Chaucer in *The Reeve's Tale*. Today we understand it to mean to quench your thirst but this wasn't always the case. There are a number of explanations for the phrase but the generally accepted one refers to apprentices who, in the past, would be sent to the local alehouse to collect a large tankard of ale for all the household. To ensure they couldn't drink any, they would be told to keep whistling as they carried it back.

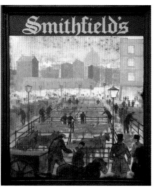

It is of no use producing goods unless you can sell them and so markets grew up to serve all the traders and, yet again, this is reflected in many pub signs such as the **Market Tavern** or **Smithfield** (for livestock markets). The buying and selling of goods requires cash and so another business developed, the banking industry; this is remembered in such names as the **Bank** and the **Exchange**.

Not all trading took place within the market. Sometimes traders needed to travel a fair distance between towns or they would wish to trade with merchants in other parts of the country. This then brought about the problem of how to move large quantities of cash around in an age when it was dangerous even for a poor man to travel. Consequently, if you wanted to move cash from one town to another in medieval times you would look for a landlord whose pub was called the **Chequers**.

Today we have a Chancellor of the "Exchequer" who is in charge of the country's finances. The term came about because, in medieval times, money would be counted out on tables marked out in a chequer-board pattern – to ease the counting of stacks of coins in regular lines. A landlord who called his pub the Chequers was therefore informing potential customers that he was prepared to carry out financial services on their behalf. So that, if you wanted to transfer funds from one town to another you could then pay your money to the landlord in your own town, he would issue you with a receipt and contact a colleague who ran a similar pub in the next town who would then pay the sum you owed to whomsoever you needed to pay. It was a most

effective system and worked throughout Europe, and is still used today in many parts of the world by those people who don't wish their funds to pass through official bodies! It wasn't just money transfers that these landlords arranged; they would often also be prepared to give loans and carry out many of those services that today we expect from our high street banks.

While on the subject of money, another interesting name is the **Tontine**. This refers to a form of investment and comes from the name of an Italian banker, Lorenzo de Tonti, who lived in the 1600s. A group of people would get together to invest in a business. Normally when this happens one would expect that on the death of each investor his investment would be inherited by his heirs.

A tontine investment, however, is different. Each member receives an annual dividend but his capital is never paid back. Quite often these agreements were used to fund public works projects. In the case of a private business it was generally agreed at the outset by all the investors that only the last surviving member of the group should inherit the business. This was done to ensure that the business was not split up at all, and ended in the hands of just one person. Inevitably in such cases, the last survivor could do very well from such an agreement and this idea has subsequently been used as a potential plot by many a mystery or detective writer.

He that drinks fast, pays slow.
Benjamin Franklin (1706 - 1790)

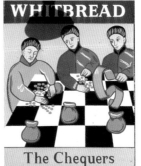

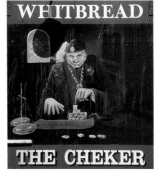

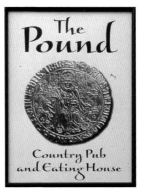

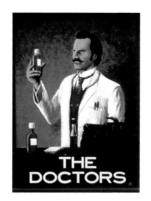

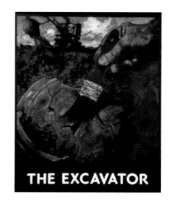

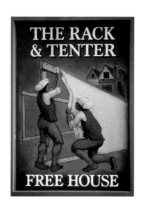

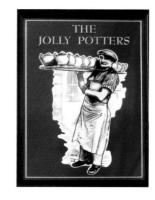

Trades old and new.

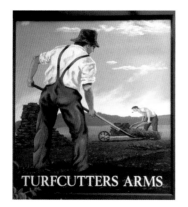

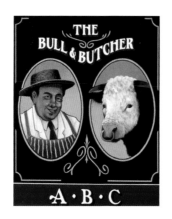

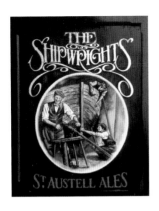

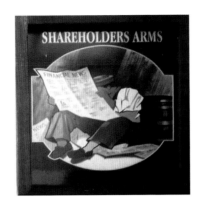

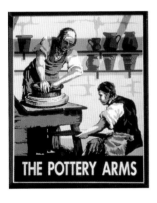

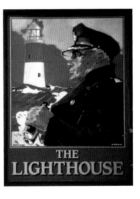

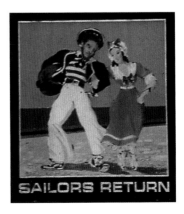

7

Transport

The road to great wine is littered with beer bottles.
Anon

The first major road system in the country was established nearly 2,000 years ago during the time that Britain was part of the great Roman Empire. Along these roads the Romans had inns regularly spaced at intervals of between 15 and 18 miles. These weren't so much for ordinary people as for those serving the Empire – messengers and tax gatherers, long-distance merchants and, in all likelihood, a few soldiers too. These inns, known as "mansios", were places where travellers could not only get food and water but also overnight accommodation and a change of horses.

With the decline of the Empire many of these old roads survived, to a greater or lesser degree. Who knows? - perhaps an occasional mansio survived on those sites where settlements had grown up around them – we may have some very old pubs indeed! But for many centuries travel for the ordinary man and woman became fraught with danger. Even once new roads were built most people would have sought the safety of travelling in numbers, stopping overnight at safe havens such as monastic houses or within towns.

It wasn't really until the 18th century that roadside inns were once again established in any numbers. In fact, the Industrial Revolution could never have happened had it not been for a vast improvement in that century of various modes of communication, enabling the newly produced goods to reach markets not just within Britain but around the world. Furthermore, as the new industries developed, people throughout the country shifted in search of the jobs that now became available.

This was a period that saw the introduction of many decent and well-maintained toll roads and canals to serve an increasingly mobile population and, to serve all these travellers, the number of inns and taverns around the country suddenly rocketed. The most obvious of the many pub signs from this time are those associated with stagecoach travel – hence you get the **Coach**, **Coach and Horses**, the

Travellers and many more. The furniture of these roads regularly gets mentioned too as, for example, with the **Milehouse**, the **Gate** or depictions of signposts.

Some stagecoaches on regular services had their own names and occasionally these also survive in the name of a pub. The **Comet** in Shrewsbury, for example, was the name given to a stagecoach that served on the route between that town and Chester. Another is the **Flying Bull** – said to be named after two stagecoaches travelling on the London to Portsmouth road, one of which was called the Fly and the other the Bull. There were also many different types of horse-drawn vehicles, and their names also survive on pub signs – the **Hackney Carriage** is one example.

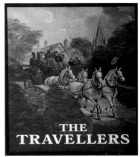

THE TRAVELLERS

THE MILEHOUSE

THE RUNNING HORSE

Occasionally, on steep hills, an additional horse would be added to the team to help pull a coach. On reaching the top, that horse would be released and would then run back of its own accord to its stable – hence the **Running Horse**.

THE BOAT

Alongside the development of decent roads was the building of a canal network that criss-crossed the country and it, too, required inns and taverns. Many of these taverns were first established to provide for the navvies working to build the canals – the word "navvy" comes from the fact that these men were building a new "navigation system" – hence the **Navigation**.

By the mid-1800s the navvies were no longer working with navigation systems but, instead, were establishing routeways for a new form of transport – the steam locomotive. Steam trains rapidly caught the imagination of people everywhere so that today they make up perhaps one of the largest types of pub sign to be found, represented all around the country. In fact, many people who collect pub signs concentrate solely on railway signs, glorying particularly in those signs where the artist has made a small mistake, usually in the way he has painted the locomotive.

AQUEDUCT INN

THE NAVIGATION INN

PUBMASTER

JAMES BRINDLEY

James Brindley and the
Duke of Bridgewater

The first canal (as opposed to a river that had just been dredged for ease of access) was built by James Brindley for the Duke of Bridgewater; the Bridgewater Canal, opened in 1761. It linked the coal mines of Worsley with Manchester and, within a year of it being opened, the price of coal in Manchester had dropped by fifty per cent.

DUKE OF BRIDGEWATER

The **Bridge** – where roads and rivers (or canals) meet there has to be a bridge. Furthermore, anyone wanting to cross from one side of a river to another will usually converge on an easy crossing point, either a ford or a bridge. There are numerous examples of pubs called the Bridge, it was naturally an excellent site for a landlord to establish his business in order to catch passing trade.

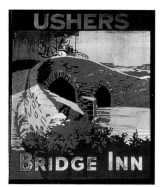
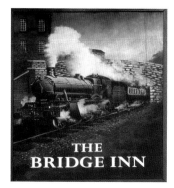

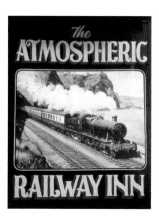
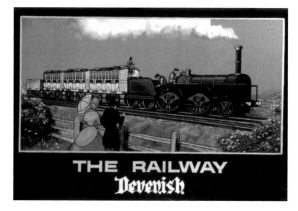
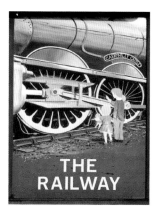

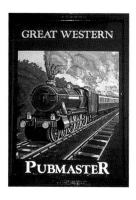

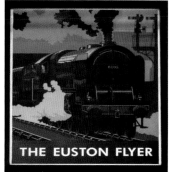

Then the 1900s saw the development of the motor car. Many of the pubs that had served the stagecoaches had suffered a decline in trade with the development of the railways but, with the growth in car ownership, particularly between the wars, they tended to recover. Today, of course, these same pubs are suffering once more with the recent laws concerning drinking and driving.

All forms of transport are to be found on signs somewhere. A subject that vies with the railways in the popularity stakes amongst pub sign collectors, is that showing various types of waterborne transport. I've already mentioned the development of the canals but, going way back in time, we have the **Coracle**; the word comes from the Latin for "leather", in other words a boat made of leather stretched around a wooden frame. Working boats of all types are represented right up to modern destroyers and liners but, without doubt, some of the finest signs around are those with sailing ships in full sail.

Incidentally, a pub called the **Anchor** may not have anything to do with ships at all – in the heraldic sense an anchor symbolised "hope" or "steadfastness"

You name it, if it's a form of transport somewhere there will be a sign with a depiction of it, from straight walking along the **Beaten Track**, being carried in a **Sedan Chair**, cycling on a **Penny Farthing** or driving in a variety of cars. Air travel isn't forgotten, from the **Air Balloon** to the **Swordfish,** and even space travel is there with "the **Eagle** has landed".

Teetotaller: One who abstains from strong drink,
sometimes totally, sometimes tolerably totally.
Ambrose Bierce (1842 – 1914)
The Devil's Dictionary

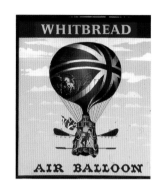

The Beaten Track

Jet and Whittle – this sign recalls Sir Frank Whittle, inventor of the jet engine. It was on 15 May 1941 (in the middle of the Second World War) that the first jet powered flight took place.

8
Political signs

Alcohol is a very necessary article… It enables Parliament to do things at eleven at night that no sane person would do at eleven in the morning.
George Bernard Shaw (1856 – 1950) *Major Barbara*

Pubs are places where people meet to chat and all sorts of subjects will come up for discussion. Today we cannot begin to overestimate the important part played by pubs as regards the development of the democracy we all now enjoy.

Let me explain. We've all found ourselves in the situation – we've just finished work for the day and, before going home, we decide to go for a quick drink with our mates, perhaps in the **Village Inn**. While we're there the conversation turns to whatever was happening in the workplace that day or news of recent events. We moan about what's going wrong, we moan about our rates of pay, we moan about how those in charge don't know what they're doing, and we generally put the world to rights. It was ever thus. Going back hundreds of years our ancestors would have been doing just the same.

One person who didn't just moan but acted as well was **Wat Tyler**. In 1381 he led a band of some 50,000 peasants from Kent to London to complain about a number of grievances, including unpopular taxes that were the same for both the very poor and the very wealthy. Meeting the King and Lord Mayor of London on Blackheath Common for a parlay, the unarmed Tyler was killed by the Lord Mayor and others. The rioting that followed caused immense damage in London

WILLIAM CAXTON

Thomas Paine – Thomas Paine's book, *The Rights of Man*, published in 1790, was to change the world. It influenced political thinking not just in this country but in revolutionary France (the French Revolution had broken out only the year before) and in the newly established republic of the United States of America. By the time of his death in 1809, 1½ million copies of the book had been sold in Europe alone.

during which the Savoy Palace was destroyed. This has come to be known as the Peasants Revolt.

Then nearly 100 years later, in 1476, **William Caxton** set up a printing press in London. (The first book he printed, incidentally, was an edition of Chaucer's *Canterbury Tales*.) The important thing about his publications was that they were printed in English. Before long other presses were producing books and then an English translation of *The Bible* was produced. The effect of this on the general public was phenomenal. Until then, only the clergy and the well-educated who could read Latin or Hebrew could read the written word of God. Suddenly it was available for anyone who could read English. People began to discuss and question what they read; it was against this background that the Reformation took place.

By the 1600s education of the masses had progressed so that around half the population was able to read and write to some extent. And then came the Civil War and discussions about politics. It's interesting to note that in 1640 22 political pamphlets were published in England; in 1642 the number had risen to 1,966. Although many people

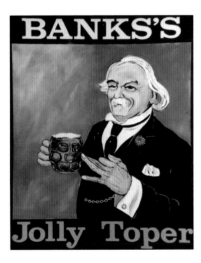

We are fighting Germany, Austria and drink, and as far as I can see, the greatest of these three deadly foes is drink.
David Lloyd George (1863 - 1945)
It was as a result of the problems with alcohol consumption during the First World War that Parliament introduced licensing hours for all public houses.

still couldn't read, these pamphlets were read aloud in meeting places such as pubs up and down the country and then the ideas within them were discussed at length.

From these pub discussions ideas moved from town to town – hence my comment that we cannot begin to overestimate the importance of pubs in the development and spread of new ideas. Then, with the Industrial Revolution of the 1700s, it was new ideas about working practices that began to be discussed – our modern trade union movement could be said to have begun in pubs, particularly since so many early pubs were closely linked to particular trades.

One particular pub sign that recalls the importance of this association between pubs and trade unions is the (Tolpuddle) **Martyrs**. Following the end of the Napoleonic Wars there was a great deal of unrest in the country. There were many reasons for this, but included amongst them was the fact that many disbanded soldiers had come home and were now seeking jobs when there were few to be had. This gave those in authority

an opportunity to lower the rates of pay. Agricultural labourers, for example, had been paid nine shillings a week. This dropped to eight shillings, then to seven, then to six. Finally six men in the village of Tolpuddle in Dorset formed a trade union and agreed, in the spring of 1834, that they would refuse to work for less than ten shillings. All six were arrested.

The trade union they had formed was, by then, perfectly legal but they had made the mistake of taking a pledge of loyalty to each other and it was on this technicality that they were charged with "administering unlawful oaths". Found guilty, all six were transported to Australia. The outcry that this caused meant that the government was obliged, two years later, to bring them all back.

Since then many political figures have featured on pub signs, not always in a complimentary fashion!

Wine is sure proof that God loves us
and wants us to be happy.
Benjamin Franklin (1706 - 1790)

Joe Arch he raised his voice, 'twas for the
working men. Then let us all rejoice and say,
We'll all be union men.
Joseph Arch was a hedge-cutter who, in 1872, founded the National Union for Agricultural Workers to set rates of pay and also get the vote for farm workers. In 1885 he became an MP.

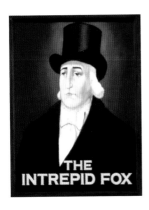

THE INTREPID FOX

THE GLADSTONE

EARL BEACONSFIELD

THE JOHN KENNEDY

AYLESBURY

THE CHURCHILLIAN

IND COOPE

CLEM ATTLEE

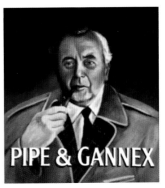

PIPE & GANNEX

Most people hate the taste of beer - to begin with. It is, however, a prejudice that many people have been able to overcome.
Winston Churchill (1874 - 1965)

FOX AND HOUNDS

9
Law and order

In vino veritas.
(Truth comes out in wine.)
Pliny the Elder (AD 23 – AD 79)

Traditionally, pubs were not just places where people met to have a drink with their friends. Simply because they were places where many people regularly met, other types of meetings were often held at such venues too. For example, minor trials and court cases were sometimes held in local pubs and many of them still recall those events in names such as the **Hundred House Inn**.

The name derives from Saxon times when counties were split up into administrative areas known as "hundreds". Administration in such areas was very much in the hands of the local lord of the manor who would also be in control of law and order within his territory and would oversee minor infringements of the law while major cases would be heard in nearby towns. Justice has to be seen to be done and so, rather than hear minor cases in the privacy of his own home, these would be held in the village inn where anyone who wished to, could attend.

The types of cases heard were those concerning perhaps, disputes over boundaries, thefts or cheating in the local market, and (a subject very close to the heart of any landowner) poaching, as illustrated here.

The case having been heard, justice would be prompt and the criminal would immediately be placed in the local **Stocks** whereupon all the "good" people of the village would use him as target practice with rotten vegetables and, in some cases, stones. Indeed, in medieval times it was stipulated by law that each village should have its own set of stocks.

Punishments were severe and many lives ended on the gallows for what were relatively minor infringements of the law and there are even pub signs that recall such times. **Sixteen String Jack** has a surprisingly happy smile on his face as he goes to the gallows. His real name was John Rann and he lived in the mid 1700s. He was a coachman, with a taste for the fine things of life, following the dandy style of dress then popular and his nickname derived from his habit of wearing eight ribbons or tassels attached to each knee of his silk breeches. Seeking to augment his income he also worked as a pickpocket, but always ensured that when he was working he was dressed very shabbily. He wasn't much good as a pickpocket, being arrested on several occasions. When his case came to court, however, he would arrive in all his finery and would subsequently be acquitted, because his accuser could never match the courtroom dandy with the shabbily dressed robber. Then, finally, he was caught with the evidence (a stolen watch) on his person. He was executed at Tyburn.

One form of punishment was **The Ducking Stool** and it's interesting to note that on this pub sign the victim being ducked is a man. It wasn't just nagging wives who were ducked. The punishment in this case appears to be for a merchant, perhaps he had been caught cheating his customers. Notice, also, the laughing townsfolk on the bridge behind.

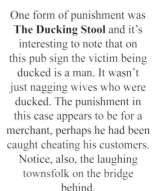

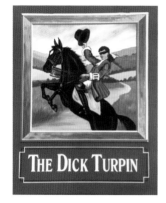

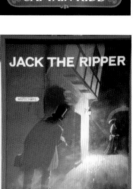

Jack is not the only criminal remembered on a pub sign. Others include **Dick Turpin**, **Captain Kidd**, even Australia's most famous criminal, **Ned Kelly**. **Jack the Ripper** is also recalled although this was one criminal who was never caught and to this day there are arguments as to his identity.

Nor is it just male criminals immortalised on signs. Amongst the women there is **Margaret Catchpole**. She and her lover were smugglers living in Ipswich. Caught by the customs officers she managed to escape by dressing herself as a sailor and stealing a horse. She rode all the way to London but was then arrested in the city and accused of horse stealing. Inevitably found guilty (she, like Sixteen String Jack, was found with the stolen property) she was sentenced to death. However, the sentence was commuted and she was instead transported to Australia where she eventually died, a well-respected citizen of the new country, in 1841.

Another lady with a dubious reputation was **Mother Redcap** who ran an inn on the Wirral. Described as "a comely, fresh-coloured Cheshire-spoken woman" who was "a great favourite with the sailor men" her inn was the haunt of local smugglers. One day, so the story goes, there was a customs officer drinking there at a time when the smugglers wanted to move goods from her cellar. How were they to get him out of the way? One of the smugglers went and lay down on the beach outside and Mother Redcap raised the alarm, saying she'd found a body on the beach. The officer went to investigate and, as he began to go through the "drowned" man's pockets seeking his identity, the "dead" man suddenly came to life and knocked him out cold. The goods were moved and then, when the officer came round the "dead" man apologised profusely for the mistake saying that he must have had a fit while walking along the beach and, when he recovered, he suddenly realised that a complete stranger was going through his pockets.

Another pub named for **Mother Red Cap** (two words in her name this time) was in Camden Town. An equally notorious lady, this Mother Red Cap had several husbands, all of whom died in mysterious circumstances. She was accused of their murders but was acquitted, although the local people were convinced of her guilt.

It's not just criminals who are remembered on pub signs – one or two lawyers get there too, although in the case of **Judge Jeffreys**, his reputation is so bad that perhaps he should be listed along with the criminals. The "Hanging Judge" or "Bloody Judge Jeffreys" became Lord Chief Justice of England aged only 33. Following the Duke of Monmouth's rebellion in 1685 he was in charge of trying all those accused of involvement and, seeking to ingratiate himself with King James II, in the course of his duties Jeffreys sentenced some 300 men to be executed, and transported a further 800 to the West Indies to slave on the sugar plantations. The Judge's own fall three years later was to rapidly follow that of the king so that, in 1688, he was thrown into the Tower of London where he later died.

Judge Jeffreys

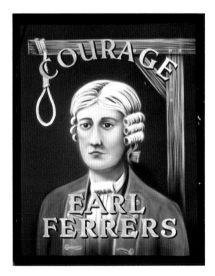

Earl Ferrers – Laurence Shirley, the fourth Earl Ferrers killed his land-steward, and was subsequently tried and condemned for murder. He was hanged at Tyburn in 1760, the last British peer to die a felon's death.

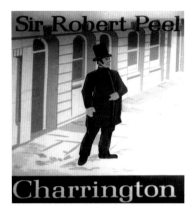

The police are the public, and the public are the police.
Robert Peel (1788 - 1850)

The 1800s saw the introduction of well-organised policing, largely as a result of the reforms introduced by Robert Peel. In 1829, as Home Secretary, Peel established the Metropolitan Police Force. One thousand constables were suddenly put on the streets of London and it was then that the nicknames of "Bobby" and "Peeler", both of course taken from Peel's names, were introduced. Although unpopular to begin with, they proved to be most effective in cutting crime. So much so that, in 1857, all cities throughout the UK were obliged to form their own police forces.

What a man says drunk, he thinks sober.
Proverb

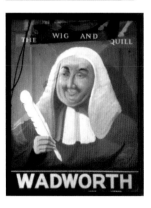

The Case is Altered – this is a pub name that goes back to the 1500s and was also used as the title of one of his plays by Ben Jonson. There are numerous explanations regarding the origin of this pub name but it's likely that it truly was used by a lawyer called Edmund Plowden (1518 – 1585) when a case he was hearing was altered following the introduction of new evidence.

10
People remembered on pubs signs

I like to have a martini,
Two at the very most.
After three I'm under the table.
After four I'm under the host.
Dorothy Parker (1893 – 1967)

The variety of people remembered on pub signs up and down the country is truly astounding. Many are instantly recognisable – monarchs, of course, are an obvious example – but it's those who are little known who are most interesting. Indeed, there are numerous people who would be totally forgotten, even in their own localities, were it not for the public houses named for them.

But not all are unknown – going back in history we have people like **Sir Walter Tyrrell** who, while out hunting in the New Forest one day, shot and killed King William II. Another person famous for his prowess with the bow and arrow was, of course, **Robin Hood**. Although he is connected in all our minds with the Forest of Sherwood in Nottinghamshire, it's remarkable how far afield we can find signs that recall him and members of his gang, such as **Maid Marion**.

Robin Hood is considered by many to be a mythical character but undoubtedly there was some outlaw living at that time who gave

rise to some of the stories associated with him. Another person considered by many to be merely a pantomime character but who was certainly real was **Dick Whittington**. There are disputes as to where he originated (probably in Gloucestershire)

SIR WALTER TYRRELL

SIR WALTER TYRRELL

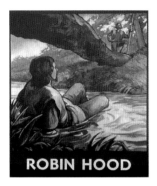

ROBIN HOOD

THE MAID MARIAN

DICK WHITTINGTON

MOTHER SHIPTON

Near this Petrifying Well, I first drew breath as records tell

CARDINAL WOOLSEY

CHARRINGTON

OLD PARRS HEAD

but Sir Richard Whittington certainly ended up as Lord Mayor of London at the turn of the 1300s and 1400s. Amongst the many benefits that he brought to London was one law he passed that prohibited the washing of animal skins in the River Thames when the weather was cold – because so many young apprentices had died as a result of hypothermia when doing so.

We certainly move back into the realm of myths when we consider **Mother Shipton** whose cavern in Yorkshire regularly draws visitors to this day. She was born in 1488 and became something of a prophetess. Unfortunately, many of her predictions weren't written down until the late 19th century, by which time events such as the defeat of the Spanish Armada and the Civil War (both of which she had predicted) had already taken place so that you are left wondering how much was written down with the advantage of hindsight.

She also predicted the dissolution of the monasteries and one person we associate with that period in history was her contemporary, **Cardinal Wolsey**. Best known today for having built Hampton Court Palace, he was one of the lucky ones who, having fallen out with Henry VIII, was on his way to London for his trial (and probable subsequent visit to the executioner's block) when he died a natural death in Leicester.

The **Old Parrs Head** sign depicts someone else who lived at this time. Thomas Parr was born in 1483 and died in 1635 – yes, those dates are said to be correct! If his biography is to be believed, he didn't marry until he was 80 years old, had an affair at the age of 100 and then, following the death of his wife, remarried when he was 122. He attributed his long life to his vegetarian diet. Invited to London to meet Charles I (he had by this time lived through the reigns of 10 monarchs) the rich food he was given was, quite literally, the death of him. He was buried in Westminster Abbey.

Thomas Parr was a soldier and many other military men are recalled – these include people such as **Clive** of India, **Admiral Benbow** and **Sir John Lawrence**. Of these, Benbow is probably only remembered by most people thanks to the pub of his name in the book *Treasure Island*; similarly Lawrence is largely forgotten today – he made a name for himself in India during the Sepoy Mutiny in the 1860s when he came to be known as the "Saviour of India". He later served as the Viceroy and Governor-General.

People of great courage are frequently remembered on signs. One lady is Grace Darling, pictured though not named, on a sign in **Bamburgh**. The daughter of a lighthouse keeper, she and her father had to make several journeys rowing out to rocks to rescue the surviving crew and passengers of the SS Forfarshire which sank in 1838. Grace died four years later of consumption which does make one wonder just how strong her health was in the first place.

Another interesting lady was **Alice Lisle**. She was arrested after harbouring rebels from the army defeated by James II's forces at the Battle of Sedgemoor in 1685. Tried by "Bloody" Judge Jeffreys, she was found guilty and executed in Winchester. Following the accession of William

Mytton and Mermaid – Jack Mytton, so the story goes, was a bit of a lad. He inherited a vast fortune while still a child and proceeded to rapidly work his way through it. He was also a bit of a ladies' man and on one occasion invited a young lady out for a ride in a boat on the River Severn. His seduction of this lady was progressing satisfactorily (indeed, they were both naked by this time) when they suddenly realised that someone was walking along the river bank and would be able to see them. In alarm Jack jumped into the river to hide himself behind the boat. Meanwhile the young lady, who couldn't swim, grabbed the first garment she could see, Jack's breeches, and tried to put them on. In her haste she put both legs down one trouser leg – hence the mermaid in the inn's name.

and Mary to the throne in 1689 her trial result was reversed – a bit late for Lady Alice, though.

Then there are quite a few ladies who can only be described as having "questionable morals" who have pubs named after them. These include people like **Nell Gwyn**, **Emma Hamilton**, Lily **Langtry** and **Marie Lloyd**. Although, unlike the others, not famous as anyone's mistress, I include Marie Lloyd in this group of ladies because of her reputation for the double entendre, accompanied with winks and rude gestures, that she used in all her songs. Mind you, when she went to the United States in 1913 she was refused entry because of her "moral turpitude". She was then still married to, though separated from, her second husband but accompanied by the man who was later to become her third husband.

If you wish to keep your affairs secret,
drink no wine.
Anon

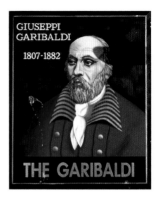

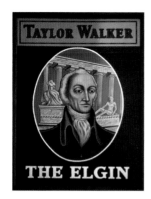

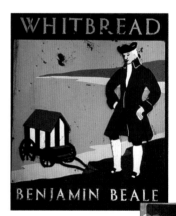

Benjamin Beale and **Martha Gunn**

Here we have two unlikely pub sign heroes, both associated with the seaside at the turn of the 18th and 19th centuries. This was a period that saw a sudden interest in seaside holidays for the wealthy, thanks largely to the physicians of the day extolling the virtues of bathing in sea water. King George III was one of the earliest such holidaymakers, he visited Weymouth on several occasions, and then his son, the Prince Regent, turned Brighton into a popular resort when he built his Brighton Pavilion.

It was in Weymouth that George III first used one of Benjamin Beale's new bathing machines. These little carriages would be pulled into the sea by horses enabling the occupants to discover "the pleasure and advantages of sea-bathing to be enjoyed in a manner consistent with the most refined delicacy".

Few people could swim in those days and ladies were particularly nervous of partaking in this new adventure and so there were people like Martha Gunn, who came to be known as "The Queen of Brighton Dippers", who would stand in the water beside the carriage steps, take hold of the ladies and gently dip them into the sea. Notice how, on the sign, she is shown standing in the water fully dressed even to her hat – that woman must have had the constitution of an ox.

11
The arts

Great literature, music or paintings are not things we would normally associate with pubs, taverns and drinking houses. Yet it's surprising how many pub signs reflect the greatest arts from our country's heritage – the art represented may not be to everyone's taste but it's still a part of our culture and heritage.

When we think of the arts on our pub signs, perhaps the first person we consider would normally be William **Shakespeare** who can be found everywhere. But he's by no means the only literary figure represented – others from much the same period in history include **Ben Jonson**, **John Bunyan** and John Milton (**Milton's Head**). From the 18th century onwards we see numerous novelists, people as varied as **Henry Fielding,** the Bronte sisters (**Wuthering Heights**) or **Edgar Wallace**.

And we shouldn't forget the poets either. From the medieval story-teller,

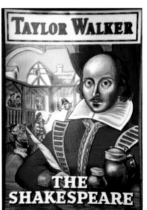

Geoffrey Chaucer who is remembered on a sign that recalls one of his *Canterbury Tales*, **The Gentil Knyght**, to **Rupert Brooke** who lies buried in Greece in a "corner of a foreign field that is forever England".

Nor are other writers ignored. The great diarist **Samuel Pepys** is there. Notice that his sign depicts a ship in the background – he was Chief Secretary to the Admiralty under both

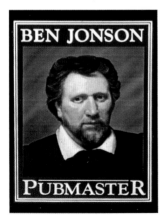

THE GENTIL KNYGHT

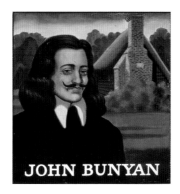

JOHN BUNYAN

Miltons Head

Bass Worthington

WHITBREAD

HENRY FIELDING

Ernest Hemingway

*Always do sober what you said
you'd do drunk.
That will teach you to keep your
mouth shut.*
Ernest Hemingway
(1899 - 1961)
The American author is probably
best known for his novels,
*A Farewell to Arms, For Whom
the Bell Tolls* and *The Old Man of
the Sea.*

George Eliot

Wuthering Heights

free house

Charlotte 16-1855   Emily 1818~1848

The Samuel Pepys

SIR WALTER SCOTT

EDGAR WALLACE

King Charles II and King James II. Another writer often featured on pub signs but who, in his case, is inevitably remembered as a war leader is Winston **Churchill** – he received the Nobel Prize for Literature in 1953, primarily for his series of books on the history of the Second World War.

Nor is it just literature that is remembered – music features a great deal. Great musicians are mentioned from composers such as **Beethoven** to players like **Louis Armstrong** and even the Beatles. More often than not, it's the musical instruments that adorn signs – these include harps, piano keys, trumpets and drums, (the last two, in particular, often showing a link with the military).

Artists too, can be found – they include **Rembrandt**, **van Dyck** and **Lowry** (pictured on a sign with one of his stick-people paintings behind him). Sometimes it's the paintings themselves that the pub is named for, as with the **Laughing Cavalier** and the Charge of the **Scots Greys**. Other signs with instantly recognisable paintings include the **Blue Eyed Maid** depicting Botticelli's *Birth of Venus* or Leonardo da Vinci's *Mona Lisa*. Interestingly, this last pub isn't known as the Mona Lisa but is called the **Third Mrs Gioconda** – her real name was Lisa di Anton Maria di Nolde Gherardini and, in 1495, she became the third wife of a certain Francesco del Gioconda.

'Tis pity wine should be so deleterious, For tea and coffee leave us much more serious.
Lord **Byron** (1788 - 1824) who was described as "mad, bad and dangerous to know".

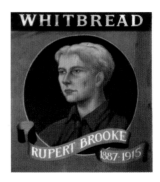

Brahms and Liszt – this is a rather amusing sign which I don't intend to explain at length. Suffice it to say that it's Cockney rhyming slang for a word that refers to someone who has had rather too much to drink.

Stars of stage and screen - some of the stars shown here are so well known that they aren't even named on the signs that depict them. How many of these examples can you name?

One man who managed to combine writing, art and music was an 18th century schoolmaster called John Collier. He wrote stories in the Lancashire dialect (much of it satirising the politics of the time), and compiled a dictionary of the dialect. He also earned money from his engraving and painting, particularly of cartoons that, once again, satirised the age. He even painted the occasional pub sign. He was also a musician, and played the flute. Because so much of his work was satirical he used the name **Tim Bobbin** as a pen name and he's remembered today on pub signs around Lancashire.

Coming more up to date there are numerous links with both stage and screen to be found on signs around the country. A number have references to the theatre, or to films and television. They include stars like Charles **Laughton** and Marilyn **Monroe**, the film director **Alfred Hitchcock** and even cartoon characters such as the **Alleycats**.

Finally, I must mention some of those pubs that have a starring role themselves in the many television soap operas. They include the **Rovers Return** in *Coronation Street*, the **Bull** in *The Archers*, the **Old Vic** in *Eastenders* and the **Woolsack** in the fictional Yorkshire village of *Emmerdale*. (The Woolsack, incidentally, is another early trade sign referring to the importance in medieval Yorkshire of the wool trade. As a reminder of the importance of the wool trade to the English economy in the time of King Edward III, the then Lord Chancellor, when sitting in the House of Lords in Parliament, would always sit on a woolsack. This tradition continues to this day although today the woolsack (or cushion) is filled with wool gathered from countries from all around the Commonwealth.) These television and radio pubs remind us of the importance of such places for social intercourse amongst the population generally; so much of the drama in each of these storylines takes place in the pub where the characters all regularly meet that it's been said that the "soap pub" has become one of the clichés of British television.

An alcoholic is someone you don't like who drinks as much as you do.
Dylan Thomas
(1914 - 1953)

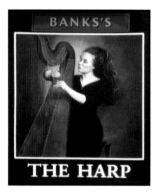

A selection of musical signs

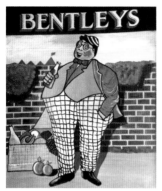

Billy Bunter

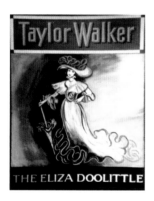

Characters from books and stories

Sherlock Holmes
Elementary, my dear Watson.
Perhaps the most famous (fictional) detective
of all times, Sherlock Holmes is also
remembered on a pub sign; believe it or not,
he never once used the phrase above in any
of the novels or short stories written about his
adventures.

12
Stories, myths and legends

Age appears to be best in four things – old wood best to burn,
old wine to drink, old friends to trust, and old authors to read.
Francis Bacon (1561 - 1628)

It's not just famous (or infamous) people who are recalled on our signs. There are numerous signs depicting people who never even existed other than in stories and, sometimes, the stories themselves. Examples of books include **Robinson Crusoe**, **Three Men in a Boat**, **Our Mutual Friend**. Children's books are recalled too with **Just William** or **The Hobbit**.

Some pubs have even been named after nursery rhymes – there's **Bo Peep** and **Simple Simon**, there's the old woman who went to the cupboard (the **Corner Cupboard**) and that man with **Seven Wives** walking "from" St Ives.

Occasionally, it's the characters from books who have pubs named for them – there's **Mr Pickwick** and **Hornblower**, **Eliza Doolittle** and **Tom Thumb**. In fact there has been more than one genuine Tom Thumb in history as it became a regular nickname for dwarfs. One example was General Tom Thumb - this was the stage name of Charles Stratton who became famous as a member of Barnum's Circus and met Queen Victoria when the circus toured in Britain. If you visit Tattershall church in Lincolnshire you'll find there the grave of another Tom Thumb.

Nursery rhymes

Jack and Jill
Jack and Jill went up the hill
To fetch a pail of water.
Jack fell down and broke his crown
And Jill came tumbling after.

Are you aware of just what you are saying when you repeat these charming nursery rhymes to small children? In actual fact this rhyme probably dates from the early 1500s and Jack and Jill, when they went up that hill to fetch water, were really disappearing to get a little privacy. The early rhyme tells us that it was Jill who broke her crown (lost her virginity) and Jack who came tumbling after – that's probably a reference to the shot-gun marriage that took place a few months later!

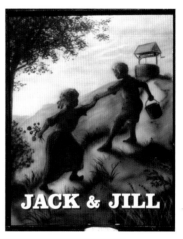

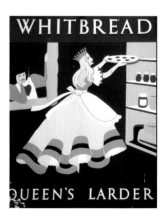

83

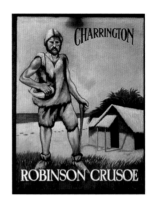

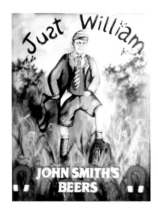

Pubs named from famous books.

You travel far, you travel near.
It's here you find the best of beer.
You pass the East, you pass the West.
If you pass this, you pass the best.
(Sign on the **Green Man**, Fownhope, Herefordshire)

There are many pubs named for legendary (or perhaps historical) figures, such as **Merlin** and the many stories surrounding King Arthur's court at **Camelot** or traditional stories such as that of the **Pied Piper**. And who is to say what stories lie behind the Cerne Abbas **Giant** or the **Long Man of Wilmington**. We do know something, however, about the **Green Man** - he's a pagan symbol of fertility and, interestingly, although he features on many a pub sign, he's often to be found in churches too.

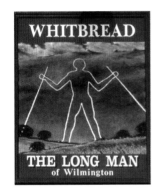

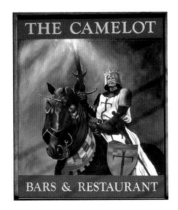

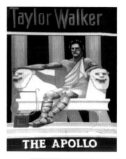

THE APOLLO

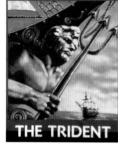

THE TRIDENT

THE MINERVA

THE GLOBE INN

HERCULES PILLARS

COURAGE

THE EUROPA

THE BACCHUS

Bacchus has drowned more men than Neptune.
Garibaldi
(1807 – 1882)

Behind much of our culture lie ancient myths and legends that our ancestors knew well. Visiting a major art gallery will remind many of us of our lack of general knowledge these days when it comes to understanding these old stories. More familiar in times past, many ancient gods feature on pub signs – Atlas can be seen holding the **Globe** on his shoulders or Hercules pushing through the mountains at the western end of the Mediterranean to form the gap between Gibraltar and north Africa otherwise known as the **Pillars of Hercules**. **Apollo**, **Europa** and **Minerva** have also had pubs named for them.

Incidentally, **Britannia** was never a goddess. The name was simply a personification of the island of Great Britain and dates back to the time of the Roman Empire. She never totally disappeared in the centuries that followed the departure of the Romans from these shores. However, she had a revival in popularity, during the 1600s and 1700s with the union of England first with Scotland and then with Ireland, when she served very much as a rallying point for all who lived in the British Isles. The accession to the throne of a young and pretty Queen Victoria did much to enhance the importance of Britannia as a symbol of the growing British Empire. Yet it was as early as 1665 that a future Duchess of Richmond posed for the figure of Britannia that subsequently graced our coins for around 300 years – she was famous as one of the few noble ladies who actually refused to become a mistress of King Charles II.

There are animals, too – **Moby Dick**, the **Cheshire Cat**, the **Owl and the Pussycat**. The famous story of the **Fox and Grapes** features on a number of signs – this probably comes about because of the association of grapes with wine and, thence, with drinking houses.

Finally there are a number of pub names that recall a particular local story. One fine example is the **Bucket of Blood** where the picture on the sign shows a man bringing up a bucket of water from his well only to find it is full of blood. The story goes that the previous night a man had been murdered and his mutilated corpse thrown down the well. This is said to be a legendary story but, in all likelihood, there's probably a kernel of truth somewhere back in the mists of time that gave rise to the pub name.

He that drinks a little too much
drinks much too much.
Proverb

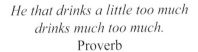

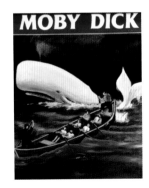

13
Natural history

Beer: Take pure spring water; the finest grains; the richest ingredients.
And then run them through a horse.
Anon

All of nature seems to be depicted on pub signs – animals and birds, fish, insects and plants (flowers, trees, even vegetables). You name it, it will be on a sign somewhere.

Animals or birds are easily identifiable and so were depicted from the earliest times. But

this wasn't necessarily simply because they made attractive pictures. More often than not, when they were shown on early pub signs they were there as symbols, usually the heraldic symbols of important people and, of course, the **Red Lion** of John of Gaunt is the best known such example. Others include the **Swan** which was often used by Edward III or Henry VIII or the **White Hart** which was the device of Richard II.

Noble families used such symbols too. The **Bear** is one example although pubs of this name can just be referring to bears being used for baiting or dancing. When linked to a colour as with the **Black Bear** or **White Bear** they often have a heraldic connection (the latter represents Earls of Kent). But the best known heraldic bear is the **Bear and the Ragged Staff** of the Earls of Warwick. There have also been variations on this with references instead to a **Bear and Rugged Staff** or to a **Bear and Billet**, a "billet" here being a thick piece of wood used as a weapon.

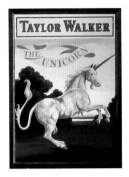

Mythical Beasts

The **Dragon** features quite often on pub signs, usually along with St George. A **Red Dragon** is, of course, associated with Wales while a **Green Dragon** was the device of the Earls of Pembroke. However, there are many other strange beasts to be found including the occasional **Unicorn**, **Griffin** or **Phoenix**.

When these signs were originally chosen as heraldic devices a great deal of thought went into the symbolism of such choices. It's a language that we are totally ignorant of today, but is fascinating nonetheless. For example, by choosing a Swan as his device Edward III was showing the world that he was learned and a lover of poetry, whilst the Bear of the Earls of Warwick showed that the family gloried in its strength and was prepared to protect those closest to it.

Dogs, of all breeds, indicated courage and loyalty. An elephant on your coat of arms showed not only that you had great strength but also possessed wit and ambition. Someone who gained power as a result of political cunning rather than prowess on the battlefield might have displayed a goat on his coat of arms or a cock, although the latter could also indicate heroism. And so it goes on.

Beehive

Within this hive, we're all alive
Good liquor makes us funny.
If you are dry, come in and try
The flavour of our honey.

There are more different species of insects in the world than the total number of all the different species of animals, birds and sea creatures put together, but you would never guess this if you judged according to their representation on inn signs. Here, however, are a few examples.

Animals, in particular, seem to fall into several categories other than as heraldic devices. Many are associated with the chase, others with agriculture and then there are numerous exotic examples as well.

Animals (and birds) associated with the chase include the **Fox** or **Fox and Hounds**, the **Buck's Head**, the **Stag** and the **Merlin** or the **Falcon**. The **White Hart** can be linked here too – there is a lovely story that tells how, out hunting on one occasion, Henry VIII came across a white stag that he wanted to shoot. The ladies who accompanied him, however, were so taken with the beauty of the beast that they persuaded him not to kill it and, supposedly, a number of pubs of that name commemorate this particular stag. Incidentally, in heraldic terms, a deer (whether buck, stag, doe, reindeer or whatever) indicates someone who will not fight unless provoked.

91

Moving on to farmyard animals we have examples of all types of farm creatures from cattle to chickens. The **Bull** or **Bull's Head** is a common enough sign, both in rural areas and in towns where they are often found close to former cattle markets. Take care with this assumption, though; as noted in Chapter Three, this name can occasionally derive from a religious Papal Bull. Incidentally, going through my own collection of Bull and Bull's Head signs I was struck by how large a proportion of these signs depict the beautiful russet-coloured Herefords with their white faces – but that may be because I live not far from Herefordshire. I leave you to discover which breeds are most commonly depicted on signs in your own area. While on the subject of coloured cattle – a "dun" cow is a brown cow and not a black and white Holstein as I once saw above a pub door.

And then there are the exotic animals from the rarely seen, though native, **Polecat**, **Badger** or **Ermine** to those of distant lands from the **Kangaroo** to the **Zebra**. The **Wolf** was once relatively common throughout Britain but became extinct in this country in the mid 1700s. One sign, the **Bleeding Wolf**, is said to commemorate the killing of the last one in Cheshire.

Another creature that was extinct here but has recently been reintroduced on the Wiltshire Downs is the **Bustard** – that pub is actually named on the Ordnance Survey map. But of all the birds shown on inn signs the most common without a doubt is the **Swan**. Look out for the **Swan with Two Necks** – this is actually a misnomer, the two necks originally were two "nicks" cut into the beaks of the birds to indicate that they were owned by the Worshipful Company of Vintners. It's assumed that the proliferation of Swan inns up and down the country came about because of this link with a trade producing so much of what was being consumed in these places.

Artichoke

There are also many signs depicting plants, with the **Royal Oak** being one of the most popular signs in the country. But you will find the occasional **Little Oak** or **Broad Oak** or even the **Acorn**. One tree to look out for is the **Yew** – being the longest lived of all our trees it was used in an heraldic sense to indicate death and eternal life. The wood from the yew was used to make bows in medieval times and in fact Henry V passed a law to protect this tree. It's not just trees either – all of nature is represented with many examples of flowers, vegetables and fruits.

Before leaving the subject of natural history I must mention a couple of individual animals remembered on pub signs. The story of

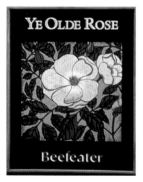

Greyfriars Bobby is well known – the little dog who, when his master died in 1858, subsequently guarded the grave for the next 14 years, leaving his post only to go to the nearby pub where he was fed. **Swansea Jack** lived in the docklands of Cardiff and is commemorated on a sign because he saved from drowning several people who fell into the sea. And does the **Jack Russell** commemorate the breed of dog or the man who created the breed?

Fear the man who drinks water and so
remembers in the morning what was said the
previous night.
Ancient Greek proverb

Creatures to be found in the water also feature on pub signs and probably the most popular of these is the **Dolphin**, heraldically a symbol of diligence, charity and love. Of the selection shown here I think my favourite is the **Lamprey** with the crown around its body, presumably reminding us of King Henry I who died as a result of eating "a surfeit of lampreys".

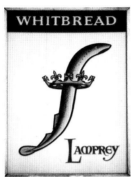

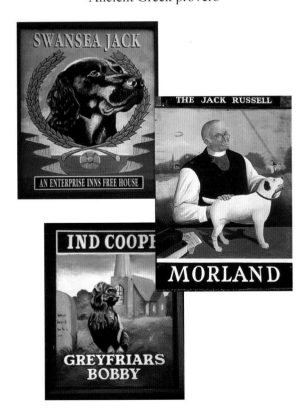

95

THE LONGBOW

WOODEN WALLS OF OLD ENGLAND

MANNS

GENERAL WOLFE
FREEHOUSE

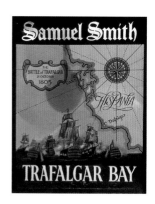

Samuel Smith

TRAFALGAR BAY

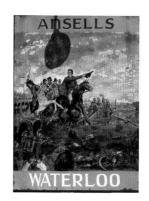

ANSELLS

WATERLOO

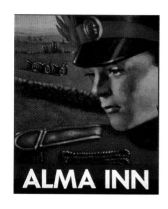

ALMA INN

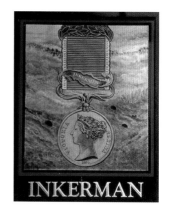

INKERMAN

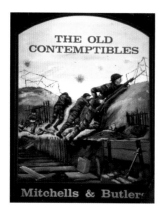

THE OLD CONTEMPTIBLES

Mitchells & Butlers

SOLDIERS RETURN

14
Warfare

Wine fills the heart with courage.
Plato (428 BC – 347 BC)

Pub signs with links to warfare are frequently to be found. Many pubs close to early battlefield sites take their names from these battles or from people featured in them. One fascinating such example is the reference to a **Swordsman** at the Battle of Stamford Bridge. Fought in 1066 (a couple of weeks before the Battle of Hastings at **Senlac** Hill) the story goes that one fearless Viking warrior held off the entire English army for some time by standing and fighting alone on a narrow bridge. Eventually one of the English soldiers waded into the river below and speared the Viking, as is rather gruesomely illustrated on the sign. With that warrior down, the army streamed across the bridge and the Viking force was defeated.

Medieval England saw constant wars against, in particular, the French. The success of battles such as those at Crécy and Agincourt depended heavily on the skill of our longbow archers, recalled on many signs. Some battles, however, were between English forces such as that at **Mortimer's Cross**, in 1461. This sign appears to show two suns seen by the combatants before the battle. This was caused by an atmospheric phenomenon when the

THE SWORDSMAN

The Archer

97

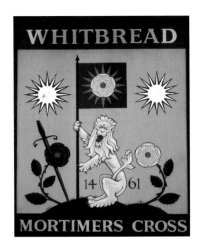

reflection from the sunlight fell on ice particles in the clouds making it look as though there was a second sun shining in the sky. The battle was subsequently won by Edward, Earl of March, later to become King Edward IV, who therefore adopted the sun as one of his symbols on his coat of arms. Notice both the red and the white rose on the inn sign, representing the Lancastrians and the Yorkists during the Wars of the Roses.

The Civil War of the 1600s is recalled on many signs, often depicting a **Roundhead** or Cavalier soldier rather than the battles themselves.

This sign remembers John **Rattlebone** who was attacked by a Viking army under King Cnut. Mortally wounded in the stomach he held a tile against his body (as pictured here) to prevent his innards from falling out and continued fighting until eventually Cnut was forced to retreat.

It is disgusting to notice the increase in the quantity of coffee used by my subjects, and the amount of money that goes out of the country as a consequence. Everybody is using coffee; this must be prevented. His Majesty was brought up on beer, and so were both his ancestors and officers. Many battles have been fought and won by soldiers nourished on beer, and the King does not believe that coffee-drinking soldiers can be relied upon to endure hardships in case of another war.
Frederick the Great of Prussia (1712 – 1786)

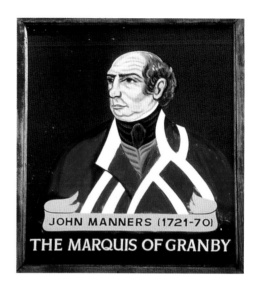

But it's from the 1700s onwards that we really see an explosion, almost, in the frequency of pub signs with military connections. A lot of this may well be thanks to the **Marquis of Granby**.

Imagine, if you will, what it was like to be a soldier serving in His Majesty's forces in the 18th century – for married men it was particularly hard to try and support a wife and children, whether they had been left behind in Britain or were with the army as camp followers. More soldiers died as a result of dysentery or other illnesses than died in battle, and in battle even relatively minor wounds could result in serious disfigurement, if not death. Then, too, it was often thought preferable for a man to be killed outright in battle than to be wounded and, perhaps, lose a limb because at least then his dependents were free to seek the support of another man.

This all caused considerable hardship and the Marquis of Granby was one of the first military leaders to recognise this problem for wounded men by giving them pensions. These were not pensions in the modern sense but a small lump

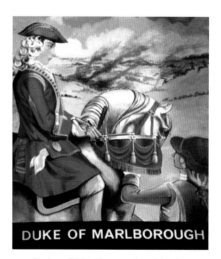

Duke of Marlborough – this sign shows John Churchill, after the Battle of Blenheim of 1704, writing a brief note to his wife in which he asked her to tell Queen Anne of his victory.

sum that could be used to help a wounded soldier set up a business of some sort. What kind of work could a wounded man take on? Well, running a small tavern was ideal – his wife could produce the food and ale, and the children could run errands and look after the customers' horses. So that many men used their "pension" to set up such a business, perhaps naming their taverns after a military engagement that they had been involved in.

The end of the century saw revolution in France and the subsequent war with the French under Napoleon Bonaparte and, of all the military themes, the Napoleonic wars feature most frequently with numerous signs depicting, particularly, Horatio **Nelson** and the Duke of **Wellington**. It's interesting to note that even **Bonaparte** himself has been portrayed on pub signs on this side of the Channel.

Then, in the mid-1800s, came the Crimean campaign so that battles such as those at **Alma**, Sebastopol and Balaclava are featured. It was at the Battle of Balaclava that the infamous Charge of the Light Brigade took place, led by **Lord Cardigan** who is remembered too. Many of the wounded from these engagements ended up in the military hospital at Scutari where they may well have been tended by **Florence** Nightingale.

Another nurse (from the First World War) was **Edith Cavell**. She was working behind German lines nursing both German and Allied soldiers and helped some 200 allied servicemen to escape to neutral Holland before being arrested and tricked into confessing. She was shot by firing squad in 1915. The night before she died she wrote "Standing as I do in view of God and eternity I realise that Patriotism is not enough. I must have no hatred or bitterness towards anyone."

In victory you deserve champagne, in defeat you need it.
Napoleon Bonaparte
(1769 – 1821)

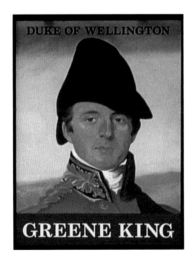

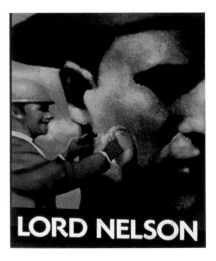

Events and people from the time of the Second World War, too, have given their names to pubs and inns. One or two particularly interesting ones stand out – such as the **Enigma**. This refers to the code breakers who worked at Bletchley Park, and developed a code breaking machine known as the Enigma in order to read the German's "unbreakable" secret code.

Our allies at the time are not forgotten either, as is evidenced by the sign depicting an American Air Force **Flying Fortress**. Many of these servicemen, along with our own **Valiant** men in the Royal Air Force suffered horrific burns when their planes caught fire, so that they required extensive treatment in the then new medicine of plastic surgery. The brave men who underwent this treatment formed what they called the **Guinea Pig** Club and even this is recalled on a pub sign.

Nor is the Royal Navy, the Senior Service, forgotten. There are numerous references to **Nelson**'s victory at the Battle of **Trafalgar** in 1805 and from then on there are signs depicting famous battleships and admirals and it's interesting to note that many of these are to be found in towns and villages that are nowhere near the coast. Incidentally, it was not just retired soldiers who ran pubs – a **Crown and Anchor** sign is often an indication that a former licencee was once a Petty Officer in the Royal Navy; the insignia comes from their arm badges.

Draft beer, not people.
Anon

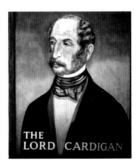

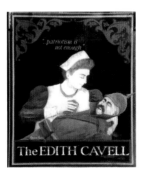

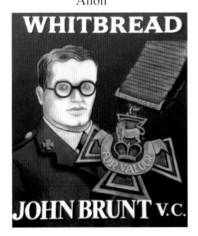

John Brunt VC - serving in Italy in 1944 with the Sherwood Foresters, his platoon came under intense mortar fire. Brunt not only held their position but he got his wounded men to safety before forcing the withdrawal of the enemy. His VC was awarded posthumously as, although he survived that engagement, he was killed the next day by a stray bullet. He was only 22.

Montgomery of Alamein

Signs from the Second World War.

15
Discovery and invention

A little bit of beer is divine medicine.
Paracelsus (1493 - 1541)

In fourteen hundred and ninety two Columbus sailed the ocean blue, and in the process he discovered America. The next century was to be a golden age of exploration, and men from all over Europe began to explore beyond the known world. This surge of exploration was very much led by England, France, Spain and Portugal and these nations constantly squabbled amongst themselves as they each tried to lay claim to as much territory as they could within the Americas. The results of this land-grab exist to this day in the languages spoken there.

Many of the men involved have since been remembered on pub signs, most often in the ports from which they sailed although this is not necessarily the case. **John Cabot** is particularly interesting because he was actually Italian (his real name was Giovanni Caboto). He settled in Bristol in 1490 and was subsequently financed by King Henry VII when he set off on his own voyage of discovery – he discovered New-found-land and thus claimed it for England. Like Columbus before him, he actually thought he had reached Asia.

Rather better-known is **Admiral** (Francis) **Drake** who was little more than a pirate. He was, however, particularly successful at stealing from the Spaniards the gold that they had already stolen

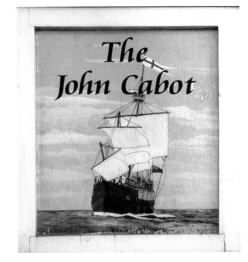

from the Incas of Mexico and so, as a result of the enormous quantities of treasure that he managed to pour into Queen Elizabeth's coffers, he sailed very much with the support of the English crown. His ship, the **Golden Hind**, has also been remembered.

Australia was subsequently discovered and much of its coastline mapped by **Captain Cook**. In Africa David **Livingstone** is remembered today very much as an explorer, although he went to the continent primarily to work as a missionary and did much to gain support for the abolition of slavery. He explored much of southern Africa and, amongst other things, he was the first European to see the Victoria Falls which he named for Queen Victoria.

Then there was Scott of the Antarctic whose ship the **Discovery** has been depicted on a sign, stranded within the ice. Another man whose ship was caught in ice was **Sir Ernest Shackleton** who went to Antarctica two years after Scott. His ship, the Endurance, was trapped and then crushed by the ice, forcing him and his crew to abandon it

and live on the ice cap. Eventually the ice broke up. Shackleton initially hoped that the ice floe on which he and his men had taken refuge would drift towards land. But it began to melt so the men had to take to their three lifeboats and sail for the nearest land. Five days later they reached Elephant Island and were able to stand on solid ground for the first time in 497 days. By then they had no supplies, and so Shackleton took the strongest of the lifeboats and set sail with five men for South Georgia, a journey of 1,300 km that took them 16 days. Landing on the south side of the island, three of the men trekked across to a whaling station on the north from where a rescue of all the crew was mounted. Perhaps the most remarkable aspect of this story is that every member of the crew survived.

Meantime, discoveries were being made in many other fields. The 18th century was to see the beginning of the Industrial Revolution and, as a result, numerous technological discoveries were made. It was in 1709 that an **Ironmaster** named Abraham Darby, working in Coalbrookdale in Shropshire, discovered how to smelt huge quantities of iron ore using coke rather than the much more wasteful charcoal. Today the great symbol of the Industrial Revolution is probably the world's first **Iron Bridge**; the bridge was erected by his grandson, another Abraham Darby, in 1779.

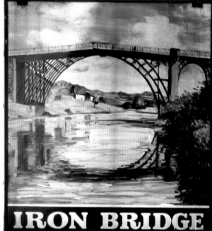

Technological discoveries came thick and fast during this period, and probably the most earth-changing of them all was the invention of Richard Trevithick's steam engine followed by the steam locomotive. The best known of the early steam locomotives was the "Rocket" built by George Stephenson, pictured as the **Engineer**, which was the winning locomotive at the Rainhill Trials in 1829. The trials were run on a stretch of railway line near the village of Rainhill between Liverpool and Manchester. Five trains took part and a prize of £500 was offered to the winning train. One by one the trains dropped out of the test leaving the Rocket as the only train to complete the trials. It averaged a speed of 12mph (although at one time it reached 30mph) and managed to haul a wagon of 13 tons.

Sir Isaac **Newton** (1642 – 1727)
If I have seen further it is by standing on the shoulders of giants.

Considered by many to have been the greatest genius who ever lived, Newton was born on Christmas Day in 1642. Today he is best known for the incident with the apple that, supposedly, instantly explained the laws of gravity to him; but he also worked with optics and mathematical principles generally. He became an MP for Cambridge University, warden of the Royal Mint and was knighted in 1705. He is buried in Westminster Abbey.

George Stephenson and his son, Robert, were given a contract to supply locomotives to the new Liverpool and Manchester Railway. Other new railway companies sprang up everywhere. One such company was the Great Western Railway (known to aficionados as God's Wonderful Railway), a leading engineer for which was Isambard Kingdom Brunel. A lesser known employee of that company, but one who is also remembered on a sign, was Sir **Daniel Gooch.** Initially its first Chief Engineer and later the Chairman of the company, he also served as Chief Engineer for the Telegraph Construction Company and so was behind the laying of the first successful telegraph cable across the Atlantic.

Along with the Industrial Revolution, the 18th century saw the period known now as the Age of Enlightenment. This could be said to have begun with Isaac Newton and continued into the early 1800s. It was a period when people began to question everything about the world around them, not just regarding the natural world but also all aspects of mathematics and science, religion and politics. All this led ultimately not just to a revolution in industry, but also to political revolutions such as that in France in 1789, and the growth in democratic ideals that followed. One group of people at the forefront of this new thinking was the Lunar Society – based in central England it included leading industrialists of the region but

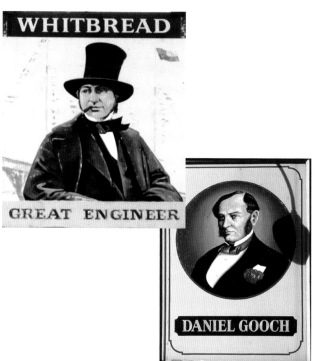

Sir David Brewster – born in 1781 in Jedburgh, Brewster was a physicist, mathematician and astronomer. Aged only 12 he was sent to Edinburgh University, his father intending that he should enter the clergy. He did, indeed, become a minister of the Church of Scotland but also followed his interests in science. He was the inventor of the kaleidoscope.

Old Dr Butler's Head – Dr Butler was a quack doctor with no qualifications whatsoever who somehow managed to become physician to King James I. On the strength of this appointment he began selling a "medicinal ale" which was only available from taverns that showed his head, hence there were at one time quite a number of pubs in London bearing this name.

its members were also in regular correspondence with scientists and thinkers (including the likes of Benjamin Franklin) in others parts of the world.

There's too much blood in my alcohol system.
Anon

Medical advances were being made too, and these are also remembered on signs. Who today has heard of **John Snow**? Yet the number of lives he has saved around the world would be too numerous ever to count. Snow was the doctor who first linked the source of a cholera outbreak in London in 1854 with a particular water pump in Soho, and so realised that it was tainted water that caused cholera.

Another man whose work has saved many lives is **Sir Alexander Fleming** who, in 1928, discovered penicillin. Lives underground were saved by the invention of the Davy lamp by **Sir Humphrey Davy** whose laboratory assistant Michael **Faraday** was also to achieve fame as a scientist – both have been remembered on pub signs.

Wine improves with age –
I like it the older I get.
Anon

If penicillin can cure those that are ill,
Spanish sherry can bring the dead back to life.
Sir Alexander Fleming (1881 – 1955)

Charles Darwin – with the publication of his book *On the Origin of Species* in 1859, Charles Darwin turned scientific thinking on its head.

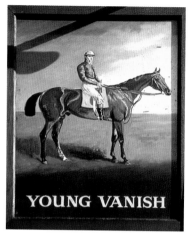

Famous Racehorses

Flying Childers is considered to be the first great racehorse in history, winning his first race in 1721 and eventually retiring unbeaten. Another great racehorse was **Young Vanish**, a steeplechaser in the 1820s and yet another pub sign racehorse was **Why Not**, the Grand National champion in 1894. The only ever dead heat in a Derby is recalled on the sign of **The Running Horses**. It was in 1828. The race was re-run and one side of the sign shows that Cadland was the winner in the end.

16
Sports and leisure activities

You don't have to be a beer drinker to play darts, but it helps.
Anon

Taverns have always been places where people went to get not only a drink, or two, but also to meet their friends, gossip and while away the time. Many a landlord through history has done his utmost to encourage his customers to stay longer and spend a little more money in his tavern and, to do this, landlords made games available for their customers to play. Today many of these games are still very closely associated with "pub culture" – games such as darts, shove ha'penny, dominos – and this tradition continues to this day with the recent introduction of pub quizzes and karaoke sessions.

One of our oldest pub names also comes from this association with gaming – the **Chequers**. In medieval times this name gained a link with money transactions as I mentioned in Chapter Six when I talked about trade signs. However, if we go back even further in time, we find the same sign dates back to the days of the Roman Empire when a landlord calling his tavern the Chequers

was indicating to potential customers that he had games available for them to play – in this case it would have been games that were the precursors of the modern draughts or chess.

As time went by many pub names also came to be linked with games, sports and leisure activities generally. Of course, these were at first

THE FOX & HOUNDS

HUNTERS INN

THE FALCON

WINFARTHING

FIGHTING COCKS

THE MORRIS MAN

Bull Ring Tavern

largely connected with what today we would call "country pursuits" and this includes many obvious names linked with hunting such as the **Hunters Inn**, the **Horse and Hound**, the **Fox and Hound**. But there are many other old activities referred to – such as the **Fighting Cocks**, the **Morris Men** or the **Maypole**.

One activity that, in the 1300s and 1400s, all men and boys over the age of seven were required by law to take part in, was archery. The need for well-trained longbow archers in the English army during the period of the Hundred Years War meant that men were expected to practice regularly at the **Butts** – this was the term given to the long, relatively narrow practice field adjacent to any town or village in the country and it survives in many street names around England.

So essential was it that all able-bodied men should practice their archery regularly, a law was once passed that banned the playing of football on a Sunday. Mind you, one somewhat bloodthirsty tradition has it that the game of football was invented during the times of Viking raids when one Viking raider was captured, beheaded and his head subsequently used as a football. In view of the almost obsessive interest by men throughout Britain in this particular sport it's surprising that there aren't numerous pub names connected to it. There are, indeed, one or two but they usually remember famous players such as **Tom Finney**, who played for England 76 times in the 1940s and 1950s.

Football is a spectator sport; on the other hand, it's generally agreed that the sport with the highest number of participants in the country is angling and, sure enough, this subject features often, from the **Jolly Anglers**, to the **Hook and Tackle**. Many of the signs associated with fishing picture a gentleman in 17th century costume and this is a direct reference to the best-known fisherman of them all, **Isaac Walton**. Born in Staffordshire, Walton became an ironmonger in London but he never lost his links with his roots, especially his love of the River Dove, his favourite fishing area. In 1653 he published his book on the subject, *The Compleat Angler, or the contemplative man's recreation*. I do so enjoy that title.

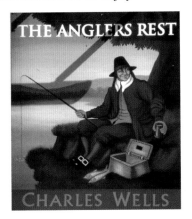

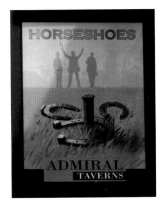

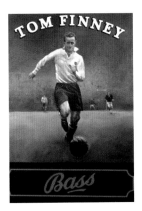

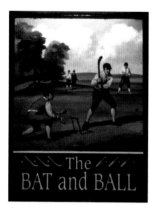

It seems to me that the sport that features most often on pub signs is cricket. It's generally agreed that this game began on the open Downs of south-eastern England using a ball made from wool or rags, which was thrown at a gate defended by someone holding a stick or bat, perhaps a shepherd's crook, hence "cricket". A game for shepherd boys at first, its rules were eventually formalised in the 1740s by players living around Hambledon in Hampshire, now seen as the birthplace of the modern game. Inevitably, a pub nearby, the **Bat and Ball** commemorates the game but there are numerous other signs depicting the sport from village to international level, many of which feature famous players amongst whom **Dr WG Grace** predominates.

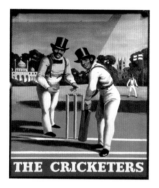

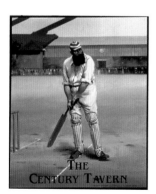

Horse and Jockey – occasionally you get a famous horse and jockey pairing as with this example. The jockey was Bob Champion and the horse, Aldaniti. Together they won the Grand National in 1981. It was one of the most popular wins ever, as both rider and horse had recently recovered from serious illness or injury, Bob Champion having had cancer and Aldaniti having recovered from an injury to his leg.

Following cricket in the popularity stakes is horse racing, from the **Starting Gate** to the **Final Furlong** or the **Winning Post**. Once again many famous riders are commemorated as at the **Champion Jockey**, in this case remembering Sir Gordon Richards, champion jockey 26 times.

One most unusual character associated with the "Sport of Kings" was **Prince Monolulu.** He wasn't a prince at all but a racing tipster and his catchphrase was "I gotta horse!" His real name was Peter Carl Mackay and although he came from Guyana he was also of Scottish descent. Between the wars, in an age before television predominated, he became something of a national icon at race meetings. He was always outlandishly dressed and, with a particularly entertaining line of patter, would offer the public his tips in envelopes that he sold as though he was a market trader.

Gold Cup

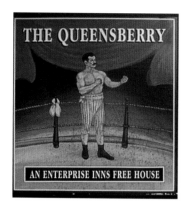

THE QUEENSBERRY

AN ENTERPRISE INNS FREE HOUSE

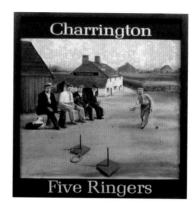

Charrington

Five Ringers

Bob Fitzsimmons World Champion 1891~99

born Helston 1863

Fitzsimmons Arms

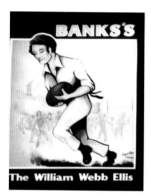

BANKS'S

The William Webb Ellis

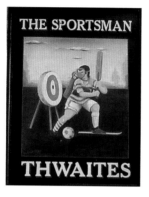

THE SPORTSMAN

THWAITES

The BOWLING GREEN

Bass

WHITBREAD

SIR FRANCIS CHICHESTER

CAPTAIN WEBB

CHEQUERED FLAG

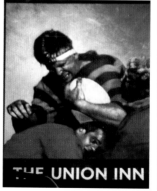

THE UNION INN

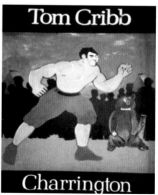

Tom Cribb

Charrington

Other racing sports include greyhound racing or athletics; there's shooting (the **Dog and Gun**), bowling (the **Bowling Green**) or rugby (the **William Webb Ellis**). Individuals include **Captain Webb** who gained fame as the first man to swim across the English Channel. He did this in 1875 and the swim took him 21 hours and 45 minutes. Another feat of endurance across the seas was the first single-handed voyage around the globe by **Sir Francis Chichester** – he completed his journey in 1967 after nine months and one day.

Boxing features quite often. There's the Marquis of **Queensberry** who, in 1867, gave his name to the rules of the sport. Famous boxers remembered on signs include **Tom Cribb**, who won his first fight in 1805. Two years later, in a fight that went on for 41 rounds, he became British heavyweight champion. Following his retirement from boxing he opened the pub that now bears his name – I bet there was no rowdiness from his customers! Another boxer, Bob **Fitzsimmons**, became the first English heavyweight champion of the world. He it was who coined the phrase "the bigger they come, the harder they fall".

Finally, one or two little-known sports must be mentioned. Did you know that the oldest annual sporting contest in the world is the Doggetts **Coat and Badge**? It's a rowing race that takes place on the Thames and began as a contest between watermen who rowed passengers across the river; it dates from 1715. Then there are the **Cheese Rollers** who congregate to race down Cooper's Hill in Gloucestershire. This race dates back at least 200 years and consists of everyone chasing down the very steep hill after a large, round Double Gloucester cheese – the local hospitals tend to be quite busy afterwards.

Indeed, just about all sports and leisure activities have, at one time or another, been represented on signs from **Gardeners** to taking a **Walk** (with) **the Dog**.

It provokes the desire, but it takes away the performance.
Therefore much drink may be said to be an equivocator with lechery.
William Shakespeare (1564 – 1616) *Macbeth*

Coat and Badge

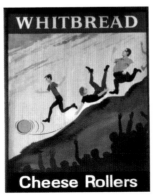

Cheese Rollers

17
The history of England in pub signs

The old inns that remain to us are, in themselves and their accumulated story, far more valuable historical monuments than our castles and abbeys. For they are not relics; they are current companions of the unbreaking pageant of the English people. They are as much a part of the social furniture of the Englishman as his home and his garden, for next to the home, no other institution has held such continuous contact with him.

Thomas Burke (1886 – 1945)

It's been said of London that the history of its taverns is the history of London, to know one is to know the other. And this applies to our pub signs, too, which throughout England reflect different periods in our history. In fact, there are so many such signs that it should be possible to write a complete history of England and illustrate it entirely with pictures taken from pub signs.

Incidentally, I use the term "England" deliberately here – although there are pictorial signs to be found throughout the British Isles, this is a tradition that is inherently an English one.

To recap on our history – firstly we go right back to the time of our **Ancient Briton** ancestors living in prehistoric times and building great monuments such as **Stonehenge**. These people lived in tribal communities often warring amongst each other and so they built strongholds known to us as hill forts such as those at Hod Hill and Maiden Castle. Unfortunately these hill forts were no defence against the military might of the Roman army that invaded **Albion** in AD 43. Despite rebellions from the likes of **Boadicea** they built roads, established towns and generally brought civilisation to us barbarians with the introduction of

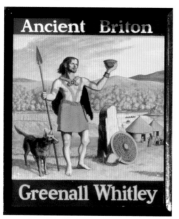

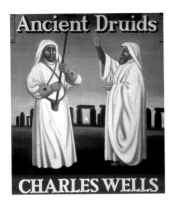

Ancient Druids
CHARLES WELLS

KING LUD

THE ROMAN LEGION
CHARLES WELLS

THE BOADICEA

THE ROMAN BATH

GREENALLS
YE OLDE DEVA

ALBION INN

SAXON KING

ST. EDMUNDS HEAD
GREENE KING

St Edmund's Head

THE DANISH INVADER

1066 – it's interesting to note the picture of Halley's Comet on this sign. It also was depicted on the *Bayeux Tapestry*. The comet was seen in the weeks just before the invasion and was considered by many to be a bad omen for King Harold as, indeed, it turned out to be when he met his death at the Battle of Hastings on **Senlac** Hill.

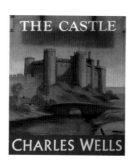

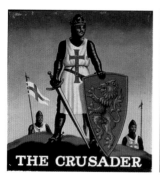

Crusaders and **Saracens**

Ale or beer was taxed in this country in 1188 when Henry II introduced a tax known as the "Saladin Tithe" to pay for the Crusades. Saladin was the greatest of the Muslim leaders and was highly respected, even by his enemies.

things like the **Roman Bath** (this pub has the remains of a Roman bath in its cellar).

In the early 5th century the Romans abandoned Britannia in order to return and defend Rome itself, leaving the country open to successive waves of Saxons, Angles, the **Danish Invader** and, ultimately, the **Norman Conquest**. These last invaders arrived in 1066, under their leader, Duke William of Normandy and proceeded to subdue us English by building **Castle**(s) throughout the land.

The centuries that followed were tumultuous and many of the events of those times are still recorded on pub signs, one of the most important of which was the signing of the **Magna Carta** by King John in 1215.

Moving rapidly through the centuries, the Wars of the Roses ended in 1485 at the Battle of Bosworth Field with victory for the Tudor king, **Henry VII**. Some of our finest portrait signs come from this period – wonderful depictions, for example, of **Henry VIII** and **Elizabeth I**. This was a period of tremendous change as regards religious thinking; it also saw an expansion in our horizons as Englishmen explored beyond the known limits of the world.

This caused friction between England and countries like Spain and culminated, in 1588, in the attack by the Spanish Armada. Warning of the approach of the Spanish fleet was flashed across the countryside using a series of **Beacons** – though not all the pub signs showing that name seem to depict that event.

Elizabeth was succeeded by James VI of Scotland in 1603 and soon after his succession we get the famous event, still remembered each 5 November, the Gunpowder Plot. Some 20 years later a number of Britons left these shores on the **Mayflower** to found a new colony in the Americas where they would have freedom to practise religion in their own way – they are known to us as the **Pilgrim Fathers**.

It was the intransigence of James's son, Charles I, that did much to cause the Civil Wars of the mid-1600s. And then 1660 saw the return to England of Charles II, an event remembered by one of the most popular signs, the **Royal Oak**.

Owen Glendower

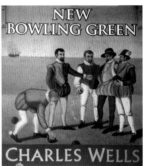

The centuries that followed saw the beginnings of the Industrial Revolution and the growth of our nation as a leader of industry throughout the world. New trades emerged, factories were built and a large proportion of the rural community travelled along the roads and canals seeking work in the rapidly expanding towns and cities. This period also saw the unification of England with Scotland and Ireland (the **Union**) and the gradual democratisation of the country so that it became a **Land of Liberty, Peace and Plenty**. All of this is recalled on pub signs. Alongside this development was the growth of a British Empire ensuring that **Red, White and Blue** criss-crossed the globe with a monarch, **Queen Victoria**, who came to epitomise the "Great" in Great Britain. All this influenced a landlord's choice of name for his inn.

Local newsworthy events are recalled on signs, also. Two I particularly like are the **Slip** in Herefordshire remembering a landslide in 1575 and the **Snowdrop** in Sussex recalling an avalanche in 1836 in which eight people were killed. The Great Fire of London of 1666 is commemorated with a pub called the **Monument**, erected afterwards and the discovery of the skeletons of **Nine Saxons** is recalled with a somewhat gruesome sign in Hampshire.

May our love be like good wine,
grow stronger as it grows older.
Old English toast

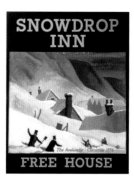

18
Pub signs around the world

Here's to a long life and a merry one,
A quick death and an easy one,
A pretty girl and an honest one,
A cold beer and another one!

Anon

Any visitor coming for the first time to these shores will have a list of places that he or she wants to visit and things to do while here and, you can be sure, that somewhere on that list will be to drink a pint of beer in a proper English inn. The "typical" public house (whatever that may be) has become an icon of all that is English and the symbol of the pub is its sign.

Similarly, when, after Christmas, you go through all the cards you have received you can be sure that somewhere in the pile there will be a card picturing a snowy scene with an "olde worlde" village inn and, outside the entrance, you will see a stagecoach with four horses and people dressed in 18th or 19th century costume. It has become a cliché but, like all the best clichés, it works because there was once a strong element of truth in the picture and it is reinforced every Christmas as we send yet more cards abroad.

It's no wonder that the pub sign is therefore seen, all around the world, as being quintessentially

English. Perhaps it is not surprising that these days when so many of us travel overseas we find that the English pub has travelled too. Wherever British tourists congregate there you will often find a "British pub" hoping to entice the tourists to somewhere where they will feel at home. Such

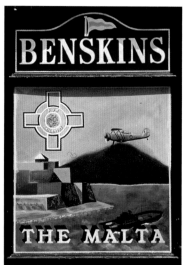

pubs can be found from Benidorm to California – usually with names such as the **King's Head**. However, one of my favourite foreign English pub signs came from a hostelry that couldn't be further from a tourist zone – the **Duck and Cover** adorns a bar serving an army barracks for the American army in Afghanistan. The date on the sign, 1387, is the Persian calendar equivalent of 2008.

But it's not just overseas that we have this foreign connection with our signs. Here in England, there are numerous signs that show links with other countries. Often they will have developed because a former landlord had an association with the named country in some way, or else the landlord is simply trying to appear more cosmopolitan.

You can travel all around the world with our pub signs – the former **Colonies** are well represented with signs reminding us of India (the **Apna Punjab**), Canada (the **Canadian Hunter**) and **Australia**. You can travel through America from New York (**Manhattans**) to Rio de Janeiro (the **Sugar Loaf**). Around Europe you can visit **Copenhagen** or **Florence**. A particularly interesting European sign is one that shows **Malta**, along with a depiction of the George Cross. This was awarded to the population of the entire island in 1942 in recognition of their courage in withstanding the German bombing that year. In fact from 1 January until 24 July there was only one 24-hour period when no bombs fell on Malta.

A fine beer may be judged with only one sip,
but it's better to be thoroughly sure.
Czech proverb

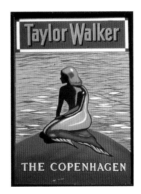
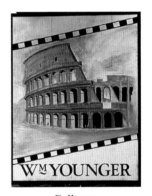

Coliseum

Kremlim – this pub is to be found in the hills of Shropshire in Titterstone Clee, an old mining community. Tradition within the region has it that the name came about because many of the locals had definite Communist tendencies during the 1950s and 1960s; not only that, it was said that the jukebox within the pub transmitted programmes from Radio Moscow, receiving the signal from a radio mast on the top of the nearby hill.

In fact the reason for the name is much more prosaic. The original name for the pub was the Craven Arms Inn which, when spoken rapidly in the local dialect, sounded almost like "Crae-ma-lin": hence Kremlin.

19
Politically incorrect pub signs

Come, come; good wine is a good familiar creature if it be well used.
Exclaim no more against it.
William Shakespeare (1564 – 1616) *Othello*

In an age when people are becoming increasingly aware of the potential to offend others through ill-spoken words, the names of some pubs are constantly being called into question. When such pubs change hands there is often a vocal minority in the neighbourhood calling for the name of the pub also to be changed; there are letters to the press, there are people holding ill-spelled banners, there are petitioners canvassing for as many names as they can …

It's a pity, really. We seem to be losing our sense of humour, particularly when we look at the history of such signs. There was never any intention of causing offence. Take the **Nag's Head** for example – there have been some particularly cruel portrayals of nagging women on recent signs. I find such signs entertaining, and please note that I am speaking as a woman.

In fact the nag on these signs has nothing to do with old women nagging their spouses. Originally, a landlord who called his inn by this name would have been advertising to the general public that he had horses available for hire. These horses would certainly never have been quality animals; they were just old nags.

One name that survives, although the illustration on the sign is usually changed, is the **Black Boy**. In most cases this sign dates from the 17th and 18th centuries when it became very fashionable for the wealthy to employ young black boys as their pages. Today, in an attempt to avoid giving offence, most of these signs will still show a young boy but he will now be a chimney sweep.

Just occasionally you will find a portrayal of King Charles II on an inn of this name. Apparently, when he was on the run following the Battle of Worcester in 1651, Charles's nickname, as he was passed from one person to another on his long road to escape to France, was "the black boy". The nickname was given to him because he had a particularly swarthy complexion.

Then there is the **Labour in Vain**. Very few of these pubs still have a picture sign because, in the past, such signs would have shown people "labouring in vain" to wash a black boy white. But, think about it. Who is the fool on such signs? It is, of course, the ignorant white woman who is trying to wash the child.

One sign that went up a few years ago and only lasted four days before it had to be withdrawn was **Tanya's Charms**. Mind you, it wasn't taken down because it was offending people. In fact, the sign was just beside a busy main road and the fear was that it would cause a serious accident.

I can't help but wonder which signs we have today, which we think are perfectly normal and inoffensive, will upset people in the future…

Warning: consumption of alcohol may cause
you to thay shings like thish.
Anon

Quiet Woman

Here's a woman
who's lost her head;
She's silent now;
you see, she's dead.

The **Compass** – sometimes alternatively known as the **Goat and Compass**, this sign is said to come from the phrase "God encompasseth us". Alternatively it can derive from the word "compassion", in which case it would appear to refer to a place where alms would once have been doled out. Then again, some people will tell you that the Goat and the Compass were originally to be found on the coats of arms of two different guilds which subsequently were amalgamated.

But, of course, compasses are also used by carpenters and masons for measurements, or by seamen to navigate – so you can choose one of many explanations when you see this sign.

20
Other interesting signs

When the wine is in, the wit is out.
Proverb

It is impossible in a book of this nature to cover all the pub signs in the country. For one thing, many come and go with astounding rapidity. Names (and signs) change all the time. Occasionally, the landlord of a pub that has locally acquired a poor reputation will want to change its name in an attempt to drop the bad reputation along with the old name.

Sometimes a landlord will change a name and then, a couple of years later, will change it back because his customers refuse to use the new name. On the other hand it can be the customers who change the name, giving their local a nickname that, perhaps years later, will become the official name. A faded pub sign for the **Golden Lion** may eventually cause the pub to become known as the **Brass Cat**. Another dilapidated pub sign for a pub called the **Golden Goblet** caused a change of name to the **Rusty Bucket**. One nickname I particularly like is the **Original Ball** (showing a globe on its sign) which was, for a time, known

locally as "Adam's Testicle" – perhaps it's no surprise that that never became official.

But, without a doubt, the best known pub nickname in the country has to be the **Dirty Duck** in Stratford-on-Avon. The official name for this pub is the **Black Swan** and visitors going there today will find that the sign is a double one with a black swan on one side and a "dirty" duck on the other; similarly these will often become "mucky" ducks.

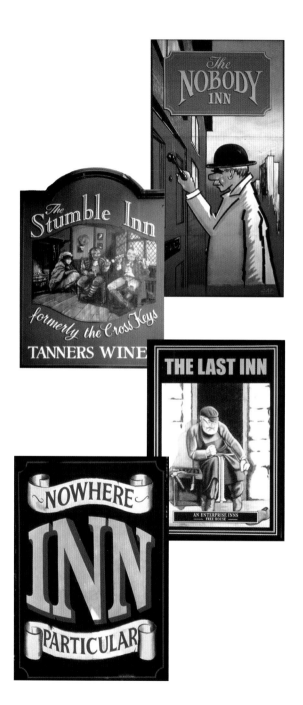

English people are renowned the world over for the way that they enjoy playing with their language. Nicknames are very much a part of this. So are puns. Examples here include names like the **Nobody Inn**, the **Nowhere Inn Particular**, the **Stumble Inn** and the **Last Inn** (this last showing a cobbler working with his last).

Then there are the pub names that have spelling mistakes – you often need to look at these twice before you see them – there's the **Cocoanut**, for example, the **Thorobred**, and the **Marlbororough Arms**. Local tradition has it that the signpainter for the last one went off for his lunch break half way through painting the sign and, when he came back, forgot how far into the word he'd painted.

Believe it or not, both the shortest and the longest pub names in the country are both to be found in the same town – Stalybridge in Greater Manchester. The shortest name is **Q** and the longest is **The Old Thirteenth Cheshire Astley Volunteer Rifleman Corps Inn** – but it's known locally as just the **Rifleman**. Another long name (the longest in London) is **I Am The Only Running Footman**. The name dates from the 1700s when footmen would run along roads ahead of their lords in their coaches, in order to clear the road and pay tolls so that gates would always be open. By the early 1800s there was only one such footman left, running for the Duke of Queensberry, and it is he who is pictured on the sign. It reminds me of those secret servicemen in the United States, running alongside the President's car.

Which is the oldest pub in the country? And do we count the age of the building or its history as a hostelry? There are several contenders for this title but the main ones appear to be **Ye Olde Fighting Cocks** in St Albans (with foundations that go back to the 8th century although the present building on top is "only" 15th century) and **Ye Olde Trip to Jerusalem** in Nottingham with a building that dates to the 1100s.

Similarly, there are arguments as to which is the smallest pub in the country – the **Nutshell** in Bury St Edmunds and the **Smith's Arms** in

Fighting Cocks

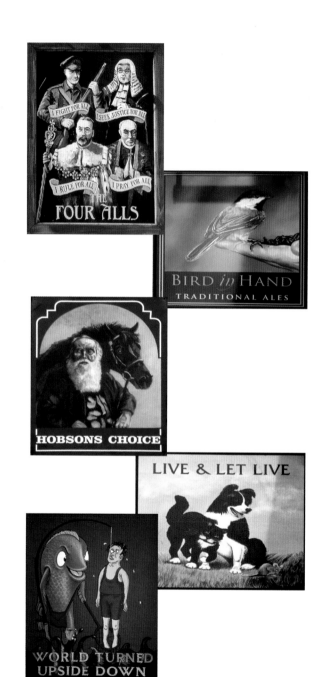

Godmanstone, Dorset, were for a long time the main claimants for this title.

Then there are unusual signs such as the **Four** (or **Five**) **Alls**. This one usually has the explanation written on the sign – there's a king (who rules over all), a lawyer (who pleads for all), a parson (who prays for all), a soldier (who fights for all) and at the end there's poor old Joe Muggins representing you and me – who pays for all. Nothing changes.

Other names come from old sayings. A landlord who calls his pub the **Bird in Hand** is reminding his customers that money in his hand is better than promises of payment to come – in other words, he won't give credit. Another is **Hobson's Choice**. Thomas Hobson lived in the 17th century and would hire out his horses in strict rotational order not allowing his customers to choose any particular animal. Another old saying is **Live and Let Live**. When life is chaotic we often speak of things being turned upside down and the illustration on the pub sign for **World Turned Upside Down** pretty well shows how we feel at such times.

Today, with so many of our pubs closing every week and their signs being taken down, we are rapidly losing one of the greatest forms of street art that we can all enjoy. May I end this book by pleading with breweries and landlords up and down the country to please do everything they can to continue this grand tradition because:

When you have lost your inns (and their signs),
drown your empty selves, for you will have lost
the last of England.
Hilaire Belloc (1870 – 1953) *The Four Men*